中国经济文库 · 应用经济学精品系列（二）

张志彬◎著
王　珺◎译

Research on Producer Services and City Economic Sustainable Development

北 京

图书在版编目（CIP）数据

生产性服务业与城市经济可持续发展研究＝Research on Producer Services and City Economic Sustainable Development：英文／张志彬著；王珺译．
—北京：中国经济出版社，2019．8
ISBN 978-7-5136-5722-8

Ⅰ．①生… Ⅱ．①张…②王… Ⅲ．①服务业—经济发展—研究—中国—英文②城市经济—经济可持续发展—研究—中国—英文 Ⅳ．①F726．9②F299．2

中国版本图书馆 CIP 数据核字（2019）第 121278 号

责任编辑　孙晓霞
英语审读　卢　炜
责任印制　马小宾
封面设计　华子设计

出版发行　中国经济出版社
印 刷 者　北京建宏印刷有限公司
经 销 者　各地新华书店
开　　本　710mm×1000mm　1/16
印　　张　18
字　　数　200 千字
版　　次　2019 年 8 月第 1 版
印　　次　2019 年 8 月第 1 次
定　　价　59．00 元
广告经营许可证　京西工商广字第 8179 号

中国经济出版社 **网址** www.economyph.com **社址** 北京市西城区百万庄北街 3 号 **邮编** 100037

本版图书如存在印装质量问题，请与本社发行中心联系调换（联系电话：010-68330607）

Preface

Since the reform and opening up, China's economy has continued to expand. In 2013, the total gross domestic product reached RMB 56.88 trillion and ranked second in the world. More specifically, the value of primary industry added to the gross domestic product was RMB 5.70 trillion and accounted for 10%. Meanwhile, the value of secondary industry added to the gross domestic product was RMB 24.97 trillion and accounted for 44%. The value of tertiary industry added to the gross domestic product was RMB 26.22 trillion and accounted for 46%. The data indicated that China has preliminarily constructed the industrial structure in accordance with the importance of developing tertiary industry, secondary industry, and primary industry. In other words, our non-agricultural industry has accounted for 90% of the gross domestic product, and China is entering a turning point in industrialisation. In 2013, the gross domestic product per capita reached RMB 41804.71, which was US $ 6747 according to the cross-country comparable price indices of the International Monetary Fund. Based on the World Bank's standards, China has become an upper-middle-income country, as the gross domestic product per capita has already exceeded US $ 6000.

With rapid economic growth, China is also undergoing the quick development of urbanisation. In 1978, the permanent population of cities and towns was only 170 million in China. By 2013, the permanent population of urban areas has reached 731 million and accounted for 53.73% of the total population, which implied that the urbanisation rate increased by 1.02% annually. It should be noted that there were 245 million migrant residents among those 731 million urban residents, accounting for about one-third of the permanent population in urban areas. In other words, according to the permanent population, China's urbanisation rate was 53.73%. However, the rate was only 35.71% if it was calculated by the population of household registration. In accordance with the population of permanent residents and those with household registration, the figures for urbanisation rate were not only far lower than the level (80%) in developed countries, but also lower than the average level (60%) in developing countries. China's urbanisation is already at a stage of rapid development, but there is still a lot of space for improvement.

In the past, the main goal of China's urban development was economic growth and the chief method was scale expansion. In this process, three super-large city groups were formed quickly, including the region of Beijing-Tianjin-Hebei, the Yangtze River Delta and the Pearl River Delta. While 18% of China's total population have been gathered in these areas which only occupied 2.8% of land area in our country, they have also created 36% of the gross domestic product for our economy. The size and number of city groups keep increasing significantly. In 2010, the number of cities was 658 in China, which was 465 more than that in 1978. There are 140 cities with more than 1 million population, accounting for 21.28% of total. More especially, six cities have more that 10 million people. Extensive expansion of urban growth relied on a large investment in material resources, but it also led to a large consumption of resources, imbalanced economic structure, serious environmental pollution, and even social conflicts. In this case, it is very hard for both the sustalnable development and the governance of the city in the long run.

Under quick development of urbanisation, the economic level and infrastructure are also increasingly improved in cities. The services and coordination of major cities will be developed gradually. Meanwhile, there is also an increasing prominent trend that companies are "withdrawing from secondary industry and entering tertiary industry" and "developing from secondary industry to tertiary industry" to change the industrial structure of economically developed cities. The importance of the service industries has increased significantly in the urban economy, especially the producer service industry, as it is highly knowledge-intensive and has close industrial linkages to other fields, takes up small space and consumes lower resources. As a consequence, the service industries have gradually replaced the manufacturing industry to be the main driving force for urban economic development and reorganisation. Therefore, it is necessary to promote the specialisation, marketisation and social development of the producer service industry, and the industry agglomeration in major cities and manufacturing-intensive areas. This will form an industrial structure based on the producer service industry in major cities and strengthen the specialised division of labor between cities to develop a multi-functional urban system comprehensively.

The history of social development since the industrial revolution shows that we must attach importance to both urbanisation and industrialisation if we want to realise modernisation of a country. The positive interaction between urbanisation and industrialisation will become an important support for China's rapid economic development in the future. Meanwhile, the development will promote the deep integration of industrialisation and information technology, and urbanisation will help develop agricultural modernisation. In the future, the strategy of "Dual Driving Force" should be implemented in division of labor and interaction for the modern manufacturing industry and producer service industry. High - end producer services will be integrated with the manufacturing industry to promote the industrial transformation and upgrading in China's economy. In addition, the development of the producer service industry is an important factor for the improvement of urban and rural residents' living standards, the acceleration of urbanisation and the transformation and upgrading of industries. In order to realise the new urbanisation, industrialisation and agricultural modernisation with Chinese features and information technology, it will be an important task to develop a sustainable urban economy for China's economic and social growth, and adjustments to a better development pattern and economic structure. In the context of economic globalisation, there are many changes in international division of labor based on the value chain now. The experience of developed countries shows that the status of cities in the global value chain can only be improved through developing advanced producer services intensively. This is not only an important way to upgrade the urban economic structure and redefine the geographical importance in the global economy, but also the basis for China to avoid falling into "middle-income traps" and realise the fundamental transformation of economic development.

As an intermediate input for other sectors and especially for industry, developing the producer service industry can improve the quality of input and invest more intellectual capital, human resources and technologies into the production process. While promoting the productivity of labor, it will also help the transformation and upgrading of industries to realise the development of China from a "large industrial country" to a "competitive industrial country". Moreover, the producer service industry is also the basic part of the urban economic system. It can increase the employment rate and income of cities and avoid the problem of "hollowing" after the slowdown of industrial development in large cities by exporting producer services to others and benefiting from multiplier effect of industrial linkages. It can also promote the development of local economic sectors and achieve the upgrading and the optimization of urban industrial structure. In order to achieve sustainable economic growth and an urban development pattern that harmonizes the environment and human beings , it is necessary to set a clear standard of "dematerialisation" in the process of urban economic growth. We should not only ensure that cities can maintain certain capacities for production, but also consider possible damages to the urban ecosystem. In this case, the ecosystem needs to keep the potential for necessary recovery. The well-known concept of "dematerialisation" requires the productivity of natural resources to increase through reducing material input by half and doubling the income or output within 50 years. The reduction in the intermediate input of capital means that producer services play a more important role in the process. This reduces not only the consumption of resources in the production process, but also the emission of pollutants at the end of production to the ecological environment, so as to improve the poor urban environmental governance in the past. Therefore, accelerating the development of the producer service industry is very important to realise the sustainable growth of urban economy and promote the transformation of China's economic development pattern in practical aspects.

This book adheres to the principle of the 12th Five-Year Plan for National Economic and Social Development of China, the Decision of the Central Committee of the Communist Party of China on Comprehensively Deepening Reforms and Several Major Issues and the New Plan for National Urbanisation Plan (2014—2020). It combines the major strategies of promoting the development of the producer service industry for the optimisation and upgrading of industrial structure and the industrial structure based on the producer service industry in big cities. I have established an in-depth understanding on the existing theoretical frameworks about urban economic sustainable development and the producer service industry. More especially, this book is mainly based on the theories about division of labor, value chain and industrial agglomeration, and the basic industrial characteristics like knowledge-intensive services, industrial linkages and intermediate investment in the producer service industry. It aims to study how these industries play a key role in the process of urban economic transformation and how they make a difference to development path and policies of the sustainable development in urban economy. From the theoretical perspective, this book explores the possibility and necessity of developing the producer service industry to promote the sustainable development of urban economy. With regard to methodology, I use analysis tools of modern econometrics and industrial economics to explain and evaluate the mechanism between the producer service industry and the sustainable development of urban economy as well as the effectiveness accurately. At the practical level, this book also provides feasible recommendations of policies to promote the development of China's urban producer service industry under the conditions of sustainable economic growth through successful cases about how to develop the producer service industry and transform the industrial structure in domestic and international cities.

Chapter 1 Literature Review

Starting from the theories of urban economic sustainable development, the literary review comments frameworks about division of labor, value chain and industrial agglomeration to analyse the theoretical basis of the rise of the producer service industry in cities, as well as the impacts on urban economic growth, the development of manufacturing industry and optimisation of spatial structure.

Chapter 2 Comparative Studies on the Development of Producer Services in Chinese and Overseas Cities

This part mainly analyses the trend and current situation of urban economic transformation to discuss the tendency of attaching higher importance to tertiary industry and urban industrial development, characteristics at different stages and the working principles. It also compares the development pattern of the producer service industry in a number of foreign and Chinese cities, such as New York, London, Tokyo, Beijing, and Shanghai.

Chapter 3 Total Factor Productivity and Regional Differences in the Producer Service Industry

This part mainly studies the differences in total factor productivity in the urban producer service industry in the eastern, central, western, northeast and other regions, including Beijing and Shanghai. It analyses the differences in the development of producer services between regions and the reasons behind. Moreover, it also explores the roles played by producer services at the different development levels of regional economies.

Chapter 4 Impacts of Developing Producer Services on Urban Industrial Transformation and Upgrading

This part mainly studies how the producer service industry improve the labor productivity and the industrial profit rate from the perspectives of economic scale and specialisation, so as to analyse the role of the producer service industry in promoting our position of industries in the global value chain.

Chapter 5 Impacts of Developing Producer Services on the Optimisation of Urban Employment Structure

This part mainly analyses the mechanism of the producer service industry to promote the optimisation of urban employment structure, including the expansion of the job market through industrial linkages, the orderly flow of labor force through the reconstruction of industrial structure and the continuous improvement of salaries through the development of the market scale for knowledge spillovers and efficient innovation.

Chapter 6 Impacts of Developing Producer Services on the Degree of "Dematerialisation" of Urban Economy

The producer service industry provides services for the production process, and the intermediate input is the essential feature. The input-output method can separate the intermediate use and the final consumption. It can also analyse how the producer service industry influences economic growth and the degree of "dematerialisation" at different stages of industrialisation.

Chapter 7 Suggestions to Promote the Development of Urban Producer Services in China

This part is mainly based on the background of sustainable development of urban economy and the differences of industrialisation in various cities to make suggestions for the development of the urban producer service industry in China. The recommendations include: optimising technological paths of industrialisation and transforming economic development patterns, promoting the reform of a market-oriented system and innovating the outsourcing pattern of services, promoting the layout of industrial clusters and improving the urban division of labor, accelerating the development of industrial integration and improving the capacity for independent innovation, regulating the ecological system and alleviating environmental pressure, etc.

This book has made academic progress in the following aspects:

(1) Under the conditions of economic globalisation and integration of information technology, the trend of attaching higher importance to tertiary industry in urban economy has become more and more apparent. Chinese metropolises such as New York, London, Beijing and Shanghai have already... including... infrastructure improvement, guidance of industrial policies, to cope with the rising cost of land and labor in China's industrialisation and provide references for the construction of a new urban system. In the post financial crisis era, export-oriented strategies, which China heavily depended for a long time, has been damaged severely. The role of a "large industrial country" has changed significantly in the pattern of globalisation. It is very urgent to transform the economic development pattern, as the pattern of economic growth has switched from exogenous to endogenous. At the urban level, export-oriented development

strategies and labor-intensive industries are facing great challenges, due to the significant increase in prices of urban land, labor and environmental protection in developed regions. Therefore, it should be the goal of China's urban economic transformation to develop the advanced manufacturing industry and modern producer service industry.

(2) This book uses the Cobb-Douglas production function and the fixed-effect model of data to measure how the total factor productivity has increased in China's service industries and the producer service industry, followowied by comparative analysis of differences between regions. The results show that the growth of productivity is relatively slow in our tertiary industry, but there is a rapid increase in the producer service industry. Moreover, the growth in the eastern region is such as Beijing and Shanghai. Faster than that in the central and western regions, the producer service industry has not only become an important force in leading the improvement of our economy, but also brought Chinese talents in the fields together for the industrial development. This book also verifies that Baumol's cost disease is only applicable to service industries but not the producer industry.

(3) By using data models of urban statistics, the empirical research on industrial development in China indicates that our industry has been at the low end of global value chain for a long time. Although labor productivity has been greatly improved by methods, such as increasing the effective management of capital and incentives for employees, it hasnot led to a simultaneous increase in profits. In central cities like Beijing, Shanghai, and Guangzhou, where marketisation is high and basic conditions are good, the producer service industry can help improve the efficiency of industrial production and achieve a significant promotion in the position of global value

chain, so as to form a functioning and specialised division of labor in cities at different levels of development. In the context of monopolistic competition, the producer service industry will increase the operating costs of enterprises. Therefore, it has no positive effects on the improvement of labor productivity in industries. The current impacts of the producer service industry on the profitability of industrial companies would mainly be the reduction of production costs by providing auxiliary services to increase profit margins. However, we still need to create better conditions for the improvement of industrial enterprises' status in global value chain.

(4) This book analyses the key role played by the producer service industry in solving the problem of employment in China. It is mainly reflected in the following aspects. Firstly, with the continuous economic development and the increasingly specialised division of labor, the industrial value chain is at the middle of further division and reorganisation, which will result in an increase in the quantity demanded for producer services and the employment rate of professionals. At the same time, the producer service industry can also help increase the overall employment rate in other industries through industrial linkages, so as to increase the total number of employees in China. Secondly, central cities and megalopolises will become the centre of urban division of labor and producer services in the process of industrialisation. Large cities will become new industrial centres, while a number of medium - sized and small - sized cities need to develop supporting facilities for them. The process of gradually improving the urban system also reflects how the labor force flows orderly and how to solve structural conflicts in the job market. Thirdly, the higher the labor productivity is, the higher wages the practioners can obtain, as the

producer service industry is at the high end of global value chain. Besides, the structural change of consumption and the upcoming increase in consumption will also lead to an increase in incomes in other industries.

(5) Based on the input – output tables of Beijing, Tianjin, Shanghai and Chongqing in 2002, 2005 and 2007, this book analyses how the development of the producer service industry influences the process of "dematerialisation" in urban economy. Through comparative analysis, the construction of the producer service industry is not only positively related to the level of urban economic development, but also favourable for the implementation of "dematerialisation" in cities. Even though certain measures have been taken to reduce the energy consumption per unit of the gross domestic product, the rebound effect caused the total emission of industrial waste gas and solid waste to remain relatively large with an upward trend. Under the extensive economic development pattern, the insufficient quantity demanded of the manufacturing industry for the producer service industry makes it difficult for the urban economy to overcome the high dependence on material resources. Consequently. it is necessary to realise the concept of "dematerialisation" in urban economy by developing the producer service industry. At this stage, the government should properly manage environmental issues and stimulate the quantity demanded for producer services to replace material input with service input.

This book studies how the producer service industry has impacts on the sustainable development of urban economy from the perspective of industrial transformation and upgrading, the optimisation of employment structure and "dematerialisation", but the development of urban producer services is not only associated with the construction of a city. It involves the development of the entire urban system and the proper and specialised division of labor among cities, so the role of the producer service industry needs to be further analysed in this process. The first question for researeh is how the producer service industry can be integrated with the industrial ecology of a city. Developing industries in an ecological way requires a high degree of coordination between urban development and natural environment to minimise material consumption by transforming to a circular economy. We still need to further study intermediate investment in the producer service industry, especially the supporting mechanism for the environmental protection. The second question is how the producer industry promotes economic growth. In addition to industrial linkages in the general sense, we should also analyse the development of China's strategic emerging industries, especially in the process of industrial transformation. We should not only help industries to upgrade, but also guide and encourage them to make changes and innovations. The third question is to discuss various parts in the producer service industry. For instance, there are also heterogeneities with different working mechanisms and development paths between the fields of financial services, modern logistics, high-tech services and business services. How to study the development of different industries under the unified production service industry is also worthy of further research and discussion.

Table of Contents

Chapter 1 Literature Review

Chapter 4 Impacts of Developing the Producer Service Industry on Urban Industrial Transformation and Upgrading

Chapter 5 Impacts of Developing the Producer Service Industry on the Optimisation of Urban Employment Structure

Chapter 6 Impacts of Developing the Producer Service Industry on "Dematerialisation"

Chapter 7 Policies for Promoting the Development of Urban Producer Service Industry in China

Chapter One

Literature Review

Urban development is closely linked to the transformation of industrial structure. At the stage of pre-industrialisation, the economy focuses on agriculture and mainly depends on geographical advantages to be a centre for distribution and commercial trade of agricultural products. At the stage of industrialisation, the city transforms into a centre of industrial economy rapidly. The current world-wide metropolises, such as London, New York and Tokyo, used to be the centre of the industrial economy and an important driving force for domestic economic growth. However, at the end of industrialisation and even the post-industrial era, the capacity of producing goods is weakening in central cities, while the capacity of providing services keeps strengthening. This clearly reflects the core competence of urban economy and determines its position in the global urban system.

Prerequisites for the development of producer services are more sufficient in cities. For example, there are well-constructed infrastructure, professional labor market and a regulated institutional environment. Therefore, companies that offer producer services tend to be clustered in cities, especially in central cities or centres of city groups. The development of the producer service industry can play an important role in promoting the quality and efficiency of urban economic growth as well as the transformation of urban economic structure. It can help adapt to the need of urban sustainable economic development under the increased global competition and constraints on resources and environmen. As a result, the key of transforming China's economic development pattern is to study the rise of the producer service industry in cities and its impacts on the urban economic development along with the national goal of keeping sustainable urban economic development. This is also an urgent problem that China needs to solve in the rapid process of urbanisation.

Chapter 1.1 The Overview of Sustainable Urban Economic Development

Chapter 1.1.1 The Introduction of Frameworks About Sustainable Economic Development

Sustainable development is an economic development path that focuses on the long term and overall planning. In 1987, "the World Commission on Environment and Development" introduced the concept of sustainable development in the report "Our Common Future" formally. It refersed to a development path that "meets the needs of the present without compromising the ability of future generations to meet their own needs". In 1992, "the World Commission on Environment and Development" agreed with the Agenda 21-a program of action for sustainable development. The plan proposed the overall goal of sustainable urban development strategies: improving not only social, economic and environmental conditions of cities, but also living and working standards for everyone. In order to promote the sustainable development of the economy and society comprehensively, our country formulated " the Program of Action for Sustainable Development in China in the Early 21st Century" in 2003 to canstitate the main ideas of sustainable development. China proposed to " consist the people-oriented and harmonious relationship between the environment and human beings, take economic development as the core with the fundamental starting point of improving people' s living conditions and innovation of technologies and systems as major breakthroughs to continuously promote the coordination of economy, society, population, resources and ecological environment in all aspects and strengthen our overall national power and competitiveness for a solid foundation for the realisation of the strategic goal at the third stage". The implementation of sustainable economic development strategies means that we need to enhance the capacity of developing the urban economy sustainably. It is necessary to accelerate the transformation of urban development patterns and optimise the spatial structure in cities to transform in intensive, intelligent, green and low-carbon directions. Meanwhile, we should make strategic adjustments to the industrial structure and spatial layout correspondingly. We can also prevent and manage "urban diseases" by enhancing the capacity of the urban economy, infrastructure, public services and resources to support the population, so as to build a harmonious, liveable, distinctive and vibrant modern city.

Chapter 1. 1. 2 The Further Study on Sustainable Urban Economic Development

From the perspective of welfare economics, the sustainable

development of urban economy means that the total welfare and welfare spending per capita cannot be reduced by time, that is, $W(t) \leqslant W(t+\Delta t)$ and $W(t)/N(t) \leqslant W(t+\Delta t)/N(t+\Delta t)$. $W(t)$ and $N(t)$ represent the total welfare and the total population respectively. $\Delta t(\geqslant 0)$ is the time increment (Daily, 1997). [1] The sustainable development of urban economy requires essentially that the economic development of a city relies on the improvement of efficiency in output rather than the increase of factors in input. It must depend on the increase in employment rate and the reduction in the gap of wealth rather than the widening income gap and impoverishment of urban residents. What's more, it should maintain the balance of the ecological environment rather than destroy it. The Urban Sustainability Index (USI), jointly published by the Urban China Initiative and the McKinsey Global Institute, is based on 23 indicators from the perspectives of the economy, society, environment and resources for calculation and analysis. In order to achieve sustainable urban economic development, scholars have conducted in-depth discussions on the meaning or standards of sustainable urban economic development from different perspectives.

(1) Efficiency in Output

From the perspective of economic growth, the sustainable development of urban economy means that the urban system emphasises on production as a key part in the process of economic development to promote the perfect combination of city's new structure and functions with the old ones for sustainable improvement of efficiency in output.

The sustainable development of urban economy and requires us to develop it in a more efficient, stable and innovative way under the premise of full use of resources. Cities should give full play to the development potential and pursue high-volume and high-quality output for social and economic growth continuously to maintain the stability of the economy the role in the urban system for the long run (Nijkamp, 1993).[2] For most cities, especially in many developing countries, cities function as an economic coordinator and a leader for industries only by improving the productivity and output of material products in cities.can We maintain core competence of the urban economy.

(2) Resource Utilisation

If we do not consider the efficiency of resource utilisation in the urban economic development, we will take the extensive economic development path which only satisfies the current needs of people in an unsustainable way.To achieve sustainable economic development, cities should rely on available resources to improve the efficiency of resource utilisation in the production process. This not only provides various material products for the current needs, but also considers the future needs of resources for survival and development.Therefore, the principle of sustainable economic development requires an ecological balance between the protection and use of resources (Walter, 1994).[3] This principle is specifically divided into three parts: "The growth rate of renewable resources used in social and economic activities shall not exceed the production rate of those resources. The rate of using non-renewable resources in social and economic activities shall not exceed the rate of developing renewable resources as a substitute. The rate of emitting pollutants into the environment in social and economic activities shall not exceed the rate of the environmental absorption and carrying capacity of pollutants" (Daily, 1997).[1]

(3) Ecological Environment

As early as 1938, Mumford (1938) began to analyse the imbalance between the nature and human beings brought by urban economic development and conducted innovative research about this question. The extensive economic development path will cause unnecessary damage to the environment. Instead, we should build an "organic city" for the coexistence and peace between the environment and urban development.[4] When Tjallingii (1995) addressed the increasingly serious problems of the urban environment that we faced, he pointed out that we could not just leave these problems to future generations or bring negative impacts on more areas and even the entire world. This would be a basic responsibility and obligation for urban development.[5] Based on this concept, Yanitsky (1987) believed that an ideal model for the sustainable development of urban economy is to achieve complete integration of the nature and technologies, maximise the creativity and productivity of labor, and improve everyone's physical and mental health and environmental conditions to the best. In this case, we should also use materials, energy and information efficiently for an ideal pattern of urban development, which is a beneficial cycle for the ecology.[6] Rigister (1987) emphasised from another perspective that cities with sustainable economic development are ecologically healthy.

They should become a business-intensive, vibrant, environmentally friendly and energy-saving centre for industrial agglomeration.[7]

(4) Social Equity

According to the Kuznets curve, it may increase the gap of wealth at the initial stage of urban economic development, which will affect the economic and social harmony of cities directly. At the social level, the ideal of sustainable urban economic development should be to build a city where human development, mutual exchange, information dissemination and cultural construction are greatly developed. We should aim to ensure the city's economic vitality, social stability and fairness of opportunities as goals of urban development. Under the trend of modern urban development, we should promote the green development of cities actively, improve the level of artificial intelligence and enhance soft power of our culture for comprehensive development of core competence in cities. Tjallingii (1995) pointed out that the social characteristics of economically sustainable cities should have these two features: ① Economically sustainable cities are also for people to live, so we should give full play to the ecological potential to provide services for healthy living conditions. We must not only consider urban areas as a whole, but also meet the needs of different people in different cities. ② Economically sustainable cities are constructed by citizens. All people and organisations, such as the public, associations, and governments, should participate in the discussion and decision-making process of urban issues and development actively.[5]

Therefore, the sustainable development of urban economy can be defined as a path of long-term sustainable urban growth and transformation of economic structure within a certain period of time and area for the combination of urbanisation and industrialisation with the use of information technology. Therefore, it meets both the current needs of urban development and basic needs of the future construction. The sustainable development of urban economy is the increase in the number of cities, the growth of size and the upgrading the structure from small to large, from low-end to high-end, from uncoordinated to coordinated and from unsustainable to sustainable (Jiang & Chen, 2003).[8] The sustainable development of urban economy is characterised by continuous improvement of efficiency in output, smaller and smaller gap of income and constant development of the environment.

Chapter 1.1.3 Working Principles of Sustainable Urban Economic Development

For the path of sustainable urban economic development, there are two mainstream thoughts based on the different focuses on technology and mechanism. One is about science and technology, and the other about policies and mechanism. On the one hand, the former usually assumes that there is an ideal system of economically sustainable cities or goals for urban economic development, relying on technical methods formulating regulations, promoting environmental protection and application of ecological technologies through policies and top-down approaches for sustainable development of urban economy. On the other hand, the latter believes that it is necessary to integrate social and commercial groups to form a competitive mechanism for environmental innovation cooperating with various interest parties to establish a partnership between governments and enterprises. It is also necessary to impose restraints on environmental damage and promote the improvement of urban ecological system and sustainable economic development through formulation and implementation of environmental policies (Guy, 1999).[9]

However, it is impossible to achieve the goal of sustainable economic development by a single approach, as the development process involves complicated circumstances in lots of aspects. According to the pressure of internal transformation and upgrading of the economy and the increasing restraints on resources and the environment, we need to implement and guide scientific policies properly for the ideal path of sustainable urban economic development. Therefore, the sustainable development of urban economy needs to combine economic transformation, scientific research, ecological technology and environmental policies effectively. When we combine the application of science and technology, we must respect the pattern of economic development and consider the actual conditions of political and social development, the principles of gradual process, flexibility and operability. It is also necessary to solve the internal conflicts between various policies and seek coordination between cities at the regional level. By fundamentally transforming the pattern of economic development, we can create the conditions for the effective achievement of sustainable urban economic development

(Bugliarello,2006).[10]

Chapter 1.2 Theoretical Bases for the Rise of the Producer Service Industry in Cities

Defining the producer service industry clearly is the foundation for the related research. However, due to the complexity and diversity, the definition of the producer service industry is not always the same. Being knowledge-intensive is the first feature of the producer service industry. Machlup(1962) was the first one to propose the concept of producer services and believed that this industry should provide various professional knowledge.[11] Browing and Singelman (1975) further emphasised that the producer service industry should provide customers with knowledge-intensive and professional services.[12] Intermediate input is the second feature of the producer service industry. Greenfield (1966) defined the producer service industry as organisations that provide intermediate goods and services for companies, non-profit institutions and governments instead of consumers.[13] Hansen(1994) argued that producer services can function as the intermediate input in production of goods and services, which would increase the value of output with higher efficiency at different stages of the production process. Hence, it would be divided into upstream activities (such as research and development) and downstream activities (such as marketing and sales).[14] From a theoretical point of view, the producer service industry refers to an industry that provides companies and other organisations with intermediate input in production activities for commercial operation and further process of production.It is not for final consumption or personal needs directly. That is to say, the producer service industry is an industry for intermediate demand rather than final consumption.Producer services are provided for the production process of enterprises and other organisations in various industries, rather than families and individual consumers. Furthermore, the producer service industry is usually characterised by high knowledge intensity, close industrial linkages and agglomeration for development.

Based on the differences between clients and the roles played in the value chain, the producer service industry is usually divided into the traditional producer service industry and the modern producer service industry. The traditional producer service industry mainly provides services for logistics and financial institutions, including transportation and warehousing, wholesale and retail, and finance and insurance. Enterprises in the traditional producer service industry mainly improve the efficiency of the production process through upgrading economic scales on the basis of dividing the industrial chain.They aim to increase the efficiency of material use in the production process. The modern producer service industry primarily provides services for the fields of information, technology and management, including information technology and computing, science and technology, leasing and business services. Enterprises in the modern producer service industry are relatively small in scale, but they provide highly customised services through putting intellectual capital and human resources into the production process. The purpose is to reduce the material input in the production process through replacing it with services. In specific studies and actual practices, there are certain differences in the definition of the producer service industry. Martinelli (1991) believed that the producer service industry would include: the service industries involved in the distribution and circulation of resources (such as banking, financial securities, logistics, and training), those involved in the design of procedures and innovation of products (such as design, research and development, project management and management of information systems), those involved in organisation and management of production (such as strategic consulting, information management, and legal financing), those involved in the production process (such as material procurement, quality control, after-sales services, and logistics management), and those involved in promotion and sales of products (such as release of new products, marketing, advertising and exhibitions, and promotion on social media).[15] Jinyong Li (2005) believed that the producer service industry would be an industry providing services as factors of production for enterprises (or organisations), including services for people, goods, wealth management, information, technology, and business operation. It would also involve many aspects, such as the flow of labor force, logistics, capital flow, information flow and technology.[16] According to "the Outline of the 12th Five-Year Plan for National Economic and Social Development of the People's Republic of China", the producerservice industry is divided into four categories-the fields of financial services (including banking, securities and insurance), modern logistics (including transportation, warehousing and postal services), high-tech services (including information transmission, computing and software, scientific research, technical services and geological exploration), and business services (including leasing and commercial services).

With the increasing competition and the deepening division of labor, a number of producer services are separated from enterprises to gather in central cities. At present, the rise of the producer service industry in cities is mainly analysed and studied from three perspectives: the division of labor, the value chain and the urban agglomeration of industries.

Chapter 1.2.1 The Division of Labor

The framework about the division of labor believes that the increasingly specialised division of labor is an important prerequisite for the development of the producer service industry. Increase in the productivity of labor is based on specialised division of labor, and the basis of that lies in the expansion of the market size. The market scale provides conditions for the division of labor, and the gradually specialised division of labor also means that the production process becomes more roundabout and the intermediate input becomes more professional and diversified. The producer service industry improves the quality of the overall production through the effects of Learning by Doing, economies of scale and knowledge spillover. The increase in specialised labor would also expand and deepen the investment of capital, so as to enhance the efficiency of production and the total output. Developing the scale of the producer service industry and the quality of output helps to reduce the production costs of enterprises and improves the competitiveness of the whole industry directly (Grubel & Walker, 1993).[17] However, the increasingly specialised division of labor would also lead to an increase in the amount, frequency and types of transactions, which may cause uncertainties of trading in the market and ethical issues in business operation. This would cause an increase in transaction costs and offset the economic benefits and the increase in labor productivity of some specialised division of labor. This requires developed service institutions to provide more professional producer services through specialised division of labor, economies of scope, institutional innovation and so on to help reduce transaction costs, enhance competitiveness and support the expansion of emerging areas in the producer service industry (Feng, 2009).[18] These emerging areas further strengthen the specialised division of labor. While satisfying the increasing demand in the market, they also promote the expansion of the producer service industry in terms of scale and variety so that the industry can be separated from the manufacturing industry to become an independent industrial sector.

According to the division of labor, the producer service industry promotes the specialised division of labor to improve labor productivity, which is an important source of modern economic growth. Economic growth helps the expansion of market scale, and the formation of specialised markets would result in the development of the producer service industry, so the cooperation between them functions well (Jiang & Liu, 2007).[19] Since the producer service industry is a contract-intensive industry, ex ante contracts and post evaluation are usually required in the production and transaction, involving more complex contractual and institutional arrangements (Wang et al., 2007).[20] Therefore, a complete market system plays a vital role in the development of the producer service industry. The standardised market mechanism of developed cities becomes the core condition that we can construct for the development and agglomeration of the producer service industry in urban areas. Major cities often have these advantages and become the centre of advanced producer services (Gu, 2010).[21]

Chapter 1.2.2 The Value Chain

According to theories of the value chain, corporate value chain can be divided into primary and supporting activities. In the entire value chain, profits at different stages are not the same. The main source of profits actually comes from certain activities through primary and supporting activities in the value chain, namely the strategic activities in the value chain (Porter, 1998).[22] Strategic activities of enterprises are mainly providing producer services at both ends of the value chain, such as research and development, design, consulting, commerce, and marketing. In the value chain, profits of manufacturing will become smaller and smaller like the "smiling curve". Therefore, companies choose to retain strategic activities in the value chain by outsourcing those activities with lower profit margins or productivity to enterprises with economies of scale and technological advantages in the producer service industry.In this way, companies can reduce costs of operation, risks of ethical misconduct in transactions and uncertainties of production.They can also allocate main resources, capital and labor on strategic activities with competitive advantages to promote innovation for higher operational flexibility and efficiency in production, so as to enhance core competence of enterprises.

The mutual promotion of activities in the producer service industry and the manufacturing industry in the value chain also promote the continuous optimisation and upgrading of urban industrial structure(Liu et al., 2010).[23] A city needs to make full use of its own dynamic comparative advantages, control strategic activities in the global integration of the value chain to seize the opportunity in the new round of transformation, and development and become the top in the global pyramid system of cities(Gu, 2010).[21] In the systematic adjustment of division of labor in the global value chain, traditional manufacturing is gradually shifted from western developed countries to developing countries. As a result, the producer service industry has developed rapidly for the enhancement of core competence in western developed countries, such as capital and securities, technological research and development, information technology, warehousing and logistics, advertising and marketing.Depending on the integration of global value chain and developing modern producer services intensively are the key factors for the successful economic transformation from a "manufacturing centre" to a "service centre" as leaders in the international system of division of labor in world-class cities, including New York, London and Tokyo (Gu & Xia, 2011). [24]

Chapter 1.2.3 The Urban Agglomeration

Since the 1990s, theories of industrial agglomeration have been extended from the manufacturing industry to the producer service industry, and the most important factor for the agglomeration of producer services in large cities would be the "face-to-face connection" between clients and companies in the producer service industry (Aguilera, 2003). [25] Firstly, it is necessary to communicate effectively between individuals through language, behaviour and non-verbal expression, as professional messages provided by the producer service industry are from computer codes (Coffey & Shearmur, 2002). [26] Secondly, it requires to reduce information asymmetry between enterprises and customers by "face-to-face communication" and transaction costs by developing trust between individuals, as industrial characteristics of the producer service industry, such as ex ante pricing and post evaluation, may lead to opportunism and ethical issues (Pandit, 2003). [27] With the development of modern communication technology, the limitations of space and time in interpersonal communication can be removed greatly, which seems to create conditions for the decentralised layout of the producer service industry and reduction in regional costs. However, the trend of concentration of producer service companies has not slowed down in major cities. On the contrary, the development of technology has also promoted the further industrial agglomeration of the producer service industry in large cities. Because the producer service industry is "fragmented", it needs comprehensive support from various enterprises in the fields like finance, logistics, commerce, research and development, so as to improve the business opportunities of the entire producer service industry and the ability of cities to integrate resources with the use of information technology.

Therefore, economic globalisation and the popularisation of information technology have promoted the strategic transformation of the manufacturing industry around the world to achieve reorganisation in terms of functions. In addition, due to factors like self-enhancement of combined effects, reputation of cities and their environment for development, producer service enterprises, especially high-end ones, are gathered intensively in world-class cities, such as New York, London, and Tokyo (Daniels, 1995).[28] Industrial agglomeration is beneficial to knowledge sharing, technological innovation, matching of specialised labor and concentration of capital, which are the basic conditions for the further development of the producer service industry.

Chapter 1.3 The Summary of Studies on How the Producer Service Industry Influences Urban Economic Development

The rise of the producer service industry in cities reflects the new trend of modern industry and urban development, and plays a key role in the sustainable development of urban economy. In addition to improving the overall development level of urban economy, it can also help the growth of the manufacturing industry and optimise the spatial structure in cities.

Chapter 1. 3. 1 Impacts of the Producer Service Industry on Urban Economic Growth

Economic development comes with a series of structural changes in industries, while the most typical phenomenon in the economic transformation and development of cities is that the employment rate increases in service industries but decreases in the manufacturing industry (Harrington, 1995).[29] In the cities with the fastest economic growth, the development of the producer service industry is also the greatest. With the rise of flexible production methods, the industrial linkages between the producer service industry and other economic sectors become closer and closer. While expanding the division of labor, it increases the efficiency in production and income levels and promotes economic development of urban economy (Hansen, 1994).[14] The contribution of the producer service industry to urban economy is mainly reflected in the following aspects. Firstly, the efficiency of economic operation and the quality of economic development can be improved through specialised division of labor. Secondly, core competence of the manufacturing industry can be improved through industrial linkages. Thirdly, industries can be transferred in an environmentally friendly way through the division of value chain to improve urban ecology and living conditions for everyone (Selya, 1994).[30]

In the process of economic development, cities often have "dependence on experience" of constructing the producer service industry and follow the development path under different national conditions. Firstly, upgrading industrial structure and spatial optimisation in urban areas can be realised for the sustainable development of urban economy through the development of the producer service industry. In this case, cities would develop in an effective way, just like London in England. Secondly, backward development of the producer service industry will cause the problem of "industry hollowing" in industries, due to the transfer of the manufacturing industry to the surrounding areas. The urban economy will begin to decline, due to the lack of new sources for economic growth, such as Detroit in the United States. Therefore, cities should create conditions for the development of the producer service industry to form agglomeration of the producer service industry. It can effectively promote the upgrading of the manufacturing industry and enhance the coordination and organisation of urban economic activities for greater capability of sustainabce urban economy development.

Chapter 1.3.2 Impacts of the Producer Service Industries on the Development of Urban Manufacturing Industry

From the industrial society to the post-industrial one, the focus of economic activities has been gradually shifted from the manufacturing industry to service-centred industries. The interaction between the producer service industry and the manufacturing industry is deepened gradually, showing a trend of interactive development. Under the assumption that specialisation led to returns to scale and monopolistic market, Francois (1990) used mathematical models to examine the relationship of interactive development between the manufacturing industry and the producer service industry.[31] Grubel and Walker (1993) also used the Austrian school's frameworks about roundabout production to explain this relationship between the manufacturing industry and the producer service industry.[17] On the one hand, economic growth, especially in the manufacturing industry, would lead to the demand for the producer service industry (Guerrieri & Meliciani, 2003).[32] Because the manufacturing industry is an important sector with high demand for producer services, many producer service companies have to rely on the manufacturing industry and provide services for the development of the manufacturing industry. However, with the development of technology, the capacity of producing goods and services in traditional manufacturings has been greatly released. When the demand does not increase correspondingly, there would be a great surplus of industrial products and profit margin would be even lowered in the manufacturing industry. As a result, various manufacturing companies begin to seek new sources to generate profits and development opportunities, and the demand for different producer services in the manufacturing industry has become higher and higher (Jiang & Liu, 2007).[19] On the other hand, the development of the producer service industry is the premise and basis for the improvement of productivity in the manufacturing industry (Mukesh & Ashok, 2001).[33] Intellectual capital, technologies and human resources included in producer services as the intermediate input can greatly improve the level of input in the manufacturing industry. It not only helps the specialisation of the manufacturing industry, but also promotes the level of specialisation and the deepening of the division of labor to improve the quality of input with lower costs in service industries. The continuous improvement of specialisation is an important way to increase labor productivity in the manufacturing industry (Liu, 2006).[34]

The core condition for the effective interactive development of industrialisation and urbanisation is the development of the producer service industry. If the producer service industry of a city is not competitive enough, it would hinder the improvement of efficiency and competitiveness in the manufacturing industry. It is reflected that labor productivity cannot be improved through specialised division of labor.

Moreover, because of the lack of support from the producer service industry, the manufacturing industry would stay at the low end of the value chain and restrict the optimisation and upgrading of the urban industrial structure and the level of economic development.

Chapter 1. 3. 3 Impacts of the Producer Service Industry on the Optimisation of Urban Spatial Structure from the Industrial Society to the Post-Industrial One

The spatial distribution of the producer service industry is more reflected as industrial agglomeration in large cities, showing the intensive development trend of the urban economy. Through the spatial distribution of division of labor, the producer service industry provides services for the interior in large cities and even the manufacturing industry outside the large cities. This is to further improve the efficiency in the manufacturing industry and promote the expansion of market to enhance the economic influence of large cities in the urban system. Coffey (1990) [35], Daniels (1995) [28], Tompson (2004) [36], Yun Zhong and Xiaopei Yan (2007) [37], Jiming Tao (2009) [38], Yiqun Zhao et al. (2009) [39] conducted research in Canada, the United Kingdom and the United States, Guangzhou, Shanghai and Beijing respectively. They all came to the conclusion that the producer service industry would be mainly concentrated in important areas of big cities or urban system. While the spatial layout of the producer service industry shows agglomeration, there is also a tendency to disperse. The heterogeneity of the producer service industry greatly affects enterprises' decisions on geographical locations. Producer service companies that can achieve standardisation tend to disperse in locations, such as logistics and finance. However, those with higher degree of customisation and no standardisation agglomerate more intensively in geographical locations, such as engineering design, management and consulting, and creative advertising (Stein, 2002).[40] Due to the agglomeration of diverse producer service companies, many small but professional central business districts would be formed in key areas of cities. In fact, the agglomeration and separate distribution of the producer service industryies are both relative. Compared with separate distribution, only when industrial agglomeration has more spatial effects, would the producer service companies be gathered to form industrial clusters and support high-end growth of urban economy. The dynamic transformation of the producer service industry in urban agglomeration and separate distribution is divided into four phases: ① Diverse companies agglomerate intensively in central business districts of cities at the early stage. ② Standardised companies are distributed separately to suburbs or the periphery of cities. ③ Companies agglomerate again in key areas of suburbs or the periphery. ④ Multi-core structure is formed in cities (Zhao & Zhou, 2007).[41]

The industrial agglomeration and separate distribution of the producer service industry promote the orderly and rational improvement of spatial layout, creating conditions for economic transformation and industrial reorganisation in cities. The producer service industry plays a leading role in spacial economy. Its influence is related to the expansion of market scale, the enhancement of corporate strength, the increase of labor income, the difference between production and management, and the technological change. Impacts of different layouts of the producer service industry in cities on urban system can be reflected through two ways: the concentration of professional labor and the division of labor between cities in terms of function. New competition around the development of the producer service industry would gradually be formed around cities in the world.

Chapter 1.3.4 Literature Review

The producer service industry involves many fields like agriculture, industry and others. As the strategic height of global industrial competition, the producer service industry is characterised by strong specialisation, innovation, high degree of industrial integration, significant driving force and so on. The development of the producerservice industry plays a vital role in transforming the economic development pattern and the urban economy. Developing the producer service industry is a major measure to adjust the dynamics of the structure and promote stable economic growth, as it can effectively stimulate the domestic demand, promote the employment rate, continuously improve living conditions and lead industries to the high end of the value chain. From the perspective of supply, the research of the producer service industry mainly focuses on how to develop the industry and form industrial agglomeration by specialised division of labor and the value chain. According to the demand, the research of the producer service industry mainly focuses on how the industry can help improve the level of manufacturing. With regards to spatial layout, the research mainly analyses how the producer service industry promotes the development of metropolises. As the world has entered the era of urbanised society and service economy, it is necessary to further analyse the mechanism for the coordinated development between the producer service industry and cities, and guide the effective development of urbanisation by making use of the situation and avoiding damages.

At present, China's urban economic development is facing the problem of structural transformation, while solving these problems is a long-term and complicated process. Future researches on the producer service industry in cities should be concentrated on the following aspects:

(1) We should study the role of knowledge spillovers in the value chain of the producer service industry. The producer service industry puts human resources and intellectual capital into the production process and strengthens the relationship between industries through the division of the value chain. The effects of knowledge spillovers would extend to the entire industrial chain, thereby improving the capability of innovating technologies in urban areas to promote the development of advanced manufacturing industry with higher efficiency in output and added value in the urban economic system. Therefore, it is necessary to combine the research of the producer service industry through the specialised division of labor to improve the labor productivity and the position in the value chain for higher industrial profits, so as to promote

technological innovation and achieve coordinated development of industrialisation and urbanisation with the use and the sharing of information technology and knowledge.

(2) We should study the impact of the development of the producer service industry on the employment rate and the income in cities. Since the producer service industry is a knowledge-intensive industry with high added value, as a basic urban sector that provides services to the surrounding areas, it can increase the income of cities through increasing the employment rate to effectively narrow the gap of income cities and industries and alleviate social conflicts. In particular, the increased employment flexibility of the producer service industry in large cities is conducive to providing more job opportunities to make the overall job market larger, guide the orderly flow of labor force, and promote the optimal allocation of the labor market. This strengthens the main functional structure of cities to closely link with regional economic development and industrial layout and adapt to the carrying capacity of the environment and resources, so as to form a scientific and rational urban structure.

(3) We should study the impact of the producer service industry on the process of "dematerialisation" in urban economy. "Dematerialisation" is a measurable target for the sustainable development of urban economy. The agglomeration of the producer service industry can reduce the spatial occupation and material dependence of cities. At the same time, producer services function as an intermediate input, so the development of the producer service industry is an alternative to material input. Therefore, it

can effectively reduce the input of resources in the production process, improve the efficiency in utilisation, decrease the degree of dependence of economic growth on materials and energy, and help reduce environmental pollution. Promoting material reduction, reuse, and utilisation of resources can improve the urban ecological environment. As a result, under the increasing restraints on the urban environment, we should fully integrate the principles of ecological development into the whole process of urbanisation through constructing the producer service industry to achieve "win-win" situation between economic development and environmental protection for a new path of urbanisation with energy conservation, intelligence, green and low-carbon concepts.

(4) We should build an overall researches framework for the producer service industry. Researches in the producer service industry began in the 1950s. Many research methods mainly depend on research in the field of manufacturing, but it has limitations in terms of methodology and it is not applicable to industrial characteristics of the producer service industry, such as diversification and specialisation. According to the basic characteristics of the producer service industry, the overall research framework for the producer service industry, including the perspectives of industrial and spatial layout, would further expand the research field, especially of various roles played by producer service companies at different levels of economic development. Therefore, specific recommendations of policies for the development of the producer service industry are proposed for coordinated and sustainable development in cities.

Chapter Two

Comparative Studies on the Development of the Producer Service Industry in Domestic and Foreign Cities

As an industry providing intermediate services, the producer service industry is characterised by high knowledge intensity and added value of products, low consumption on resources and low envirinmental pollution, which is useful to maintain the continuity of the priduction process and promote the sustainability of the production process and promote the sustainability of technological progress and the possibility of increasing efficiency in production. With the current international competition, the acceleration of capital flow cross countries, the international transfer of the manufacturing industry, and the reorganisation of the division of labor in global industries, there is an increasing trend of industrial agglomeration, globalisation of research, development with higher use of information technology in the manufacturing industry and more concentration on services in economic system. The service economy has replaced the manufacturing economy as the main driving force for economic development in the developed countries. The agglomeration and the development of the producer service industry in cities play an important role in alleviating pressure of urban resources and the environment, improving economic services, enhancing the strategic position of global value chains and comprehensive competitiveness to be the main driving force for urban economic transformation in the post-industrial era. For these goals, the development of producer service industry should be taken as a strategic focus to promote the transformation of China ' s urban economic development pattern and adjustment and upgrading of industrial structure, so as to form an industrial structure led by the producer service industry gradually. Under the economic globalisation, it would create opportunities for the successful realisation of the urban economy from an extensive development pattern to an intensive one for the strategic economic transformation from a "manufacturing centre" to a "service centre".

Chapter 2.1 The Urban Economic Transformation and Development of the Producer Service Industry

As an important spatial carrier of human economic development and social progress, cities accommodate 50% of the population and 80% of the gross domestic product with 2% of land area in the world. However, cities also occupy 85% of the world's energy consumption, emit the same amount of greenhouse gas and withstand uncountable environmental pollution and a large number of the poor population (Li & Liu, 2011).[42] Pressure from energy, the environment, and the society forces cities to change the current economic development pattern to achieve economic transformation. The transformation and development of urban economy is that cities should establish a perfect modern industrial system through industrial and spatial reconstruction and enhance the international competitiveness of urban industries under market economy. The essence is the process of repositioning and reshaping urban functions in the global division of labor network, which includes the replacement of traditional industries by newly emerging industries, low-end industries by high-end industries, and low-tech industries by high-tech industries (Wu & Li, 2010).[43] The expansion of economic globalisation and the increasingly specialised division of labor require cities to rely on the development of the producer service industry with new technologies, products of high added value and strong industrial linkages for the upgrading of urban industrial structure, the optimisation of spatial layout, the enhancement of core competence in urban areas and the transformation of urban economic structure.

Chapter 2.1.1 The Trend and the Practical Engagement of Urban Economic Transformation

The experience of urban development in developed countries shows that urban economic transformation is often directly related to the economic cycle of recession and prosperity. The transformation of modern industrial economy is consistent with the Kondratieff Wave for 50 to 60 years (Xu, 1997).[44] This is also consistent with Schumpeter's theory of economic cycles based on technological innovation. That is, the economic cycle is the result of new-round technological innovations. The economic prosperity would continuously increase the level of urbanisation and lead to strategic adjustment of urban pattern in the world (Schumpeter, 1939).[45] Under the background of economic cycle, technological advancement and urbanisation, cities usually transform from resource-based or location-based to manufacturing-centred and then to service-oriented. At the early stage of economic development, cities are often developed through the comparative advantages of resources and location. Driven by the industrial revolution, capital and labor continue to be gathered in cities to develop the manufacturing industry, which makes cities become a centre of the industrial economy. As the economy develops in depth, cities cannot afford greater agglomeration, and "urban diseases", such as, overpopulation, traffic jams, shortages of resources and environmental pollution, start. Manufacturing companies begin to distribute to more cities, and the producer service industry, including finance, information, research and development, and marketing, is gradually separated from the manufacturing industry by "outsourcing services" to become the most important driving force for urban economic development. The agglomeration and the development of the producer service industry in cities further promote the orderly and rational improvement of spatial layout for the economic transformation in urban areas. Due to different levels of urbanisation, the economic transformation is not the same in every city and the process may be tough and long, but it is inevitable in development.[46]

(1) The industrial revolution (from the 1780s to the mid-19th century) began in the United Kingdom and originated in the central area of England. As an early stage of industrialisation with capitalism, the industrial revolution completed the transformation from handicraft workshops to factories with machines. It is a revolution of production and technology that replaces manpower by machines and replaces production of large-scale factories by individual handicraft workshops. Therefore, the period of industrial revolution was also called the "machine age". Steam engines drove the development of looms, air blowers and milling machines, which promoted the rapid development of

textile, printing and dyeing, metallurgy and mining. Although agriculture was still the mainstay of the economy, the ratio of the manufacturing industry began to increase significantly. The United Kingdom completed the bourgeois revolution and become the most developed capitalist country in the world. What's more, London become an international central city and the centre of the global economy. The process of global urbanisation just started at this stage and the urbanisation rate only increased from 3% in 1789 to 6.4% in 1849, but the rate reached 50% in the United Kingdom, making it the the first country to achieve urbanisation basically.

(2) The first technological revolution (from the mid-19th century to the end of the 19th century) took place in more regions and changed the pattern of global economic and urban development. The industrial revolution led to the rise of machinery manufacturing, steel industry, transportation industry and other industries in several countries, and preliminarily formed a complete system of modern industrial technology in Western capitalist countries. The importance of the manufacturing industry became a leading industry, while agriculture was less emphasised and became a subsidiary. The era of industrialisation has already come. The economy of the United States seized the opportunity of the technological revolution, and the global central cities gradually began to shift from London to New York.

(3) The second technological revolution (from the late 19th century to the 1950s) allowed more emerging capitalist countries in the Western, such as Germany and Japan, to participate in the global

economic competition. There were also two world wars during this period. Despite this, the revolution of electricity led to the rise of a large number of technology-intensive industries, such as electricity, electronics, chemistry, automobiles and aviation. Cities entered the era of electrification from the era of mechanisation, and infrastructures were greatly improved. The manufacturing industry became the mainst of urban economy, and the proportion of service industries also started to increase. New York and London were at the top of the global urban system.

After the first and second technological revolutions, the rate of global urbanisation rose from 6.4% in 1849 to 28.4% in 1945. However, urbanisation mainly occurs in developed capitalist countries, and the urbanisation rate has reached 50% for basic achievement of urbanisation. The proportion of urban population is only 16.2% in developing countries, which just enter the initial stage of urbanisation.

(4) The third technological revolution (from the 1950s to the end of the 20th century) made breakthroughs in the fields of atomic energy, electronic computing, microelectronics, aerospace technology, molecular biology and genetic engineering. The manufacturing industry in developed countries began the high-end enhancement, and the gross value and employment rate started to decline. Manufacturing companies began to shift to developing countries gradually. The producer service industry became the mainstream of urban economy as the important support for the development of high-end technology. Traditional capitalist countries still dominate the global economy, with New York,

London and Tokyo, as triangle global urban system.

(5) The fourth scientific and technological revolution (from the end of the 20th century to the present) resulted in the development of bioinformatics, biochips, bio-solar, biological computing and so on. The era of information has come. The emerging producer service industry drives and dominates the urban economic development gradually. Developed cities like New York, London, Tokyo and Paris, are still dominating the global economy, but a large number of cities have emerged in the process of the globalisation of information technology. Cities in emerging industrial countries, such as Beijing, Shanghai, China-Hong Kong, Seoul and Singapore, have risen rapidly, and the global urban development has entered a stage of adjustment.

With the promotion of the third and fourth basic revolutions and the rise of developing countries, the rate of global urbanisation rose from 28.4% in 1945 to 50% in 2008. The urban population has surpassed the rural population for the first time, marking the beginning of the urban society. It should be pointed out that the urban population of developed countries has exceeded 70% and entered the stage of urban economic transformation, so these countries pay more attention to the quality of urban development and the trend of "ecological industrialisation" with "economic services" is becoming more and more obvious, at the stage of accelerating development led by industrial cities. The urban population of developing countries has also exceeded 40%.

With the development of economic globalisation, especially after the international financial crisis in 2008, the global economy is undergoing intensive adjustment for a new layout. Because of external and internal factors, cities are forced to face the pressure of economic transformation.

Firstly, globalisation and the popularisation of information technology have caused profound changes in the international division of labor. Globalisation has led to the worldwide flow and reorganisation of capital, technology and labor, which made the location of different activities in the production process more separate. The division of the industrial chain and the deepening specialisation have promoted the high concentration of the producer service industry within big cities, thus promoting the urban transformation and forming new division of labor in the global urban system. At the same time, developed countries have entered the post-industrial era through the popularisation of information technology. The improvement of infrastructure and the revolution of information technology have promoted the commercial development of various specialised services. With the knowledge economy as the key, service industries have become the mainstream of the economic structure. Developed countries use their capital, technology and talents to dominate the transformation of the international division of labor through economic globalisation, so as to strengthen the control of the global industrial chain.

Secondly, we need to promote a fundamental shift in the way of how to develop the economy, because of energy and environmental pressure. The rapid development of cities has brought not only economic growth but also energy consumption and ecological pollution. On one hand, in order to maintain a high level of welfare, the consumption of energy and resources per capita remains high in developed countries. On the other hand, due to scientific and technological limitations, economic growth in developing countries would consume more energy and other natural resources inevitably. The global pressure of environmental pollution and shortages of resources is increasing day by day, which would encourage cities around the world to jointly seek a path of sustainable economic development.

Thirdly, the deepening process of urbanisation has driven the urban economic transformation. According to the S-shaped urbanisation curve, when the urbanisation rate is less than 30%, it is the initial stage of urbanisation. When the urbanisation rate is from 30% to 70%, it is the stage of accelerating development. When the urbanisation rate is higher than 70%, it would enter the stage of stable development. This is a process of transforming from extensive development to high-end enhancement (Northam, 1979).[47] At present, the urbanisation rate of developed countries is above 70%, which is in the stage of stable development of building service-oriented cities. In 2013, China's urbanisation rate also reached 53.73%, which represented the stage of accelerating development. Urbanisation is transformed from the extensive development of population growth and spatial expansion to the continuous optimisation of high-end urbanisation. When the comprehensive, coordinated and sustainable development becomes a strategy of urban development, transforming urban economy becomes an inevitable option.

Finally, cities will become the most important spatial carrier for participating in the international division of labor to achieve sustainable economic development. Cities, instead of countries, are mostly influenced by globalization; cities therefore become the frontiers for a country or region to seize opportunities of globalisation and cope with risks and challenges correspondingly. Cities function as an important area of organisation for a country or region to participate in the international division of labor, reflecting the comprehensive economic competitiveness. The 21st century is the era of global urbanisation and urban globalisation. This would lead to the strategic adjustment of major cities in the world, which will further affect the path of urban economic transformation.

Chapter 2.1.2 The Trend of Attaching Higher Importance to Tertiary Sector in Urban Industrial Development

The 21st century is the era of global urbanisation and urban globalisation. As typical areas with economic functions, cities are considered to be the most economically vibrant region. With the advancement of information technology and the increasingly specialised division of labor, functions of cities are beginning to change from organisation of production to industrial management and coordination. In the past, cities were supported by traditional industries, but it was transformed to the advanced manufacturing industry and modern producer service industry. The continuous construction, deconstruction and reconstruction of urban industrial structure is also the process of spatial development in urban industries. The indication of this process is the continuous agglomeration and proliferation of industries.

At the early stage of urban development, cities often depend on resources, labor, land, location and other comparative advantages to develop the manufacturing industry intensively. Through gathering factors of production continuously to form industrial clusters, cities can gain external economies, such as knowledge spillovers, economies of scale, market of specialised labor and industrial linkages, so as to make it the centre of manufacturing and the industrial economy (Marshall, 1890).[48] The operation of industrial clusters and the division of the value chain would lead to the increasing level of complexity in specialisation. The "expansion of division of labor between industries" and "deepening division of labor within an industry" would lead to the development of enterprises in different industries or at various stages of specialisation in the same industry (Yang, 1994).[49] As the economy develops in depth, if the scale of resource consumption is further expanded, it may exceed the carrying capacity of the environment. The increase in costs of production and transaction makes it less efficient for manufacturing enterprises to agglomerate in urban development. "Urban diseases" are becoming more and more prominent, such as overpopulation, traffic congestion, resource shortages, and environmental pollution. When the environment, land and public facilities cannot afford any more, manufacturing companies with dependence on the scale of factors in production would move to areas with lower costs of land and labor.

In the process of distributing manufacturing companies to outer areas, the producer service industry is gradually separated from manufacturing by "outsourcing services" to form independent organisations of producer services and promote the further development of urban economy. In order to maintain competitive advantages, some manufacturing companies outsource non-strategic activities with less added value in the production process through "outsourcing production" or "providing services of manufacturing" to realise the transformation from a manufacturing enterprise to a producer service enterprise. The specialisation of the producer service industry makes production more efficient through the effects of Learning by Doing and economies of scale (Jiang & Liu, 2007).[19] Cities would gradually develop into an industrial structure based on the agglomeration of service economy. Through putting technology, intellectual capital, human resources and other advanced factors into production by producer service enterprises that agglomerate in central areas, production would be more roundabout and specialised with deepening investment of capital to promote industrial reorganisation effectively (Grubel & Walker, 1990) it is difficult to standardise.[17]

Compared with the manufacturing industry, it is more difficult to standardize the producer service industry, as it is more dependent on human resources, knowledge and technology. Therefore, developing the producer service industry can become a more stable and long-lasting source of competitive advantages for cities, and it would be the mainstream of industrial development in urban areas inevitably (Oliva, 2003).[50] The producer service industry forms a "centralised layout" in the economic centre of cities. That is to say, the producer service industry is agglomerated in cities, but companies are categorised by specialised division of labor to distribute in different regions, so both of industrial agglomeration and separate distribution can exist at the same time. Trading activities that involve uncomplicated and standardised services tend to be separate in spatial layout, while those involving complex and customised services tend to agglomerate (Stein, 2002).[40] In the process of sustainable urban development, the capabilities of agglomerating and distributing the producer service industry are promoted mutually for the orderly and rational spatial layout of urban industries. As a result, the urban industrial reorganisation would be completed and the economic position would be improved (see Figure 3.1).

The trend of urban industrial development is to form an industrial structure based on service economy, and the producer service industry is the most important part. It is also the organisational carrier for the transformation of production pattern from industrialisation to service, and is the basis for reconstruction of urban industries (Hall & Pain, 2009).[51] Firstly, the producer service industry is conducive to coordinating and managing specialised production processes and achieving economies of scale. The producer service industry reduces costs of manufacturing, making transactions through specialised division of labor, economies of scope and institutional innovation to support the new expansion of the manufacturing industry in terms of improvement in added value and core competence (Feng, 2009).[18] The process of urbanisation is also closely linked to the agglomeration and proliferation of service industries. The status and functions of a globalised city are fundamentally supported by the global influence of multinational corporations that establish offices in local areas, and the basis for this support is the developed producer service industry. Secondly, the producer service industry improves the labor productivity and the capability of absorbing the labor force by expanding the division of labor. The rise of the producer service industry is based on profound adjustment of the urban industrial structure under the trend of economic globalisation with the popularisation of information technology. This adjustment guarantees the space for the development of the producer service industry in urban areas, and thus achieves the improvement of labor productivity and employment rate by attracting a large number of specialised employees. Finally, the producer service industry adapts to the rise of flexible production methods, which are opposite to Fordism's standardised mass production. The essence of flexible production methods is customisation and on-demand production, requiring each company to focus on a specific phase of production and specialise it to obtain unique core competitiveness. From the nature and tasks of production, these enterprises constitute a complete industrial chain in order to minimise costs and the producer service industry intensively agglomerates in cities around the industrial chain.

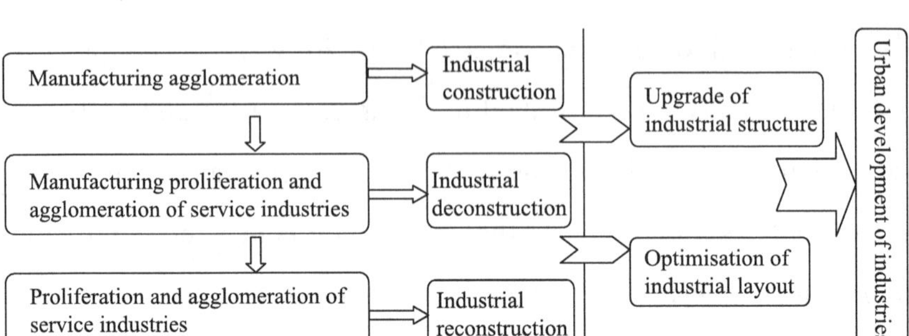

Figure 2.1 Industrial agglomeration, proliferation and urban development of industries

As the producer service industry is a "fragmented" industry under the highly specialised division of labor, there is a need for diversified companies to support each other, and the capability of attracting customers by individual companies is very limited. Therefore, a number of producer service companies with the same nature would work together and form an industrial cluster with a relatively large scale of market, greatly improving the capability of attracting customers. In this way, the producer service companies in industrial agglomeration can develop the external economy, such as saving transaction costs and increasing business opportunities, so as to make up for the high operating costs caused by expensive rents and salaries for professional workers. When enterprises in service industries are geographically too intensive, there will be a number of uneconomic effects of agglomeration, which will lead to a shortage of professional employees and the insufficient public facilities to meet the development needs, and eventually a gradual decline in production efficiency. The development of information technology would cause some producer service companies to gradually weaken the dependence of customers' geographical location and move to the outer area of cities. At this time, agglomeration does not occur in a single place but in complex centres of cities, that is, the producer service industry agglomerates by various categories in urban areas.

Chapter 2.1.3 Characteristics of the Development of the Producer Service Industry at Different Stages

With the advancement of industrialisation, profits in the manufacturing industry would decrease gradually, so industrial enterprises must rely on the support of the producer service industry in order to obtain higher added value and greater core competence for transformation and upgrading. With the development of the producer service industry, the trend of "providing services of manufacturing" or "service-oriented manufacturing" is becoming more and more obvious. However, the transformation of industrial structure is gradual at different levels of urban economic development, so the role of the producer service industry is not always the same. The development of the producer service industry is usually divided into three stages: seed stage, development stage and maturity stage, which function as the "coordinator", "driving force", and "booster" respectively (Lv, Liu & Wang, 2006).[52]

(1) Seed stage is the early stage of industrialisation. At this stage, manufacturing enterprises agglomerate in cities and become the mainstay of urban economy. Manufacturing companies' various needs of

producer services are satisfied internally, as there has not been an external market for producer services to support the requirements of the manufacturing industry. The producer service industry mainly focuses on traditional industries, such as transportation, logistics, post and telecommunications, and finance, and provides important auxiliary services for industrial production. It is a subsidiary and "coordinator" to improve the operational efficiency of various industries or production activities in the production process.

(2) Development stage is the late stage of industrialisation. At this stage, the manufacturing industry is developing rapidly, and knowledge-intensive and technology-intensive manufacturing companies have extensive quantity demanded on the producer service industry for intermediate steps in the production. Internal activities of manufacturing enterprises gradually begin to "externalise", and the external market of producer service would be formed gradually. The producer service industry plays a very important role in promoting rapid development of the manufacturing industry and accelerating the process of industrialisation. With the expanding scale of manufacturing enterprises and the increasing competition in the international market, and especially the development of high-end technology, internal service projects of companies are separated continuously, leading to rapid development of the industries that provide business services, such as advertising, consulting, intermediary, and marketing. At the same time, research and development, e-commerce and other emerging areas of producer services have also made great progress. Through knowledge

spillovers and technological innovations, the producer service industry would help the "productivity" of urban economy to increase significantly.

(3) Mature stage is the post-industrial society. In the post-industrial society, the urban economy would change from "manufacturing economy or industrial economy" to "service economy". The producer service industry would develop in an all-round way and become more and more mature to replace the manufacturing industry and function as the main "booster" for urban economic development. After entering the maturity stage, the market segmentation of the producer service industry and the level of specialisation of services are higher, and there are not only standardised services, but also customised and innovative services. The industries, such as financial insurance and business services, would be further developed. Furthermore, modern knowledge-based service industries would accelerate the development for the mainstream business trend, such as technological research and development, information services, and education and training.

With economic development and the transformation of urban industrial system, the role of the producer service industry continues to be enhanced in the urban economic system. It is inevitable to form an industrial structure led by producer services in the development of cities and especially metropolises. For a country, good conditions can only be created through institutional innovation and optimisation of the market environment for the agglomeration and development of the producer service industry with strong industrial linkages, high knowledge intensity and low dependence on resources in cities. This can resolve the bottlenecks of resources and the environment effectively, improve the ability of scientific and technological innovation, and develop new advantages in industrial competition. As a result, a number of cosmopolitan cities with comprehensive economic competitiveness would be developed to switch to a better position of the global value chain, participate in international cooperation and division of labor at a higher level, and share the fruits of economic globalisation.

Chapter 2.1.4 The Mechanism of the Producer Service Industry in Promoting Urban Economic Transformation

As the core of modern service industries, the producer service industry is an important part to study the transformation of urban economic structure. The producer service industry is the booster of urban economic development. Its development can effectively promote the upgrading of urban industrial structure, optimisation of layout, improvement in innovation capacities and alleviation of resources and environmental pressure to enhance industrial competitiveness for sustainable urban economic development.

(1) The producer service industry can accelerate the development of industrial integration and promote the upgrading of urban industries. The producer service industry has strong industrial linkages as the intermediate input in the development of other industries, and it can accelerate the integration of various industries, extend the urban industrial chain, expand the space for industrial development and

promote the optimisation and upgrading of urban industrial structure. On the one hand, the producer service industry can carry out technological advancement of low-end processing and manufacturing industries in cities. Urban traditional processing and manufacturing industries tend to rely heavily on labor and land, so the pressure on resources and environmental pollution is high. However, low-tech activities result in low production efficiency. In the process of urban economic transformation, transforming and upgrading low-end processing and manufacturing industries with the producer service industry is an important way to adjust the industrial structure of cities. The producer service industry can put knowledge-intensive elements into the production process to improve the proportion of high-end, efficient and high value-added industries in the traditional manufacturing industry. It plays an important role in improving the efficiency of industries, improving the quality of development and optimising the internal structure. On the other hand, the producer service industry would infiltrate knowledge into high-tech industries and modern manufacturing industries. The producer service industry like software and computing, would infiltrate modern manufacturing industries gradually, greatly enhancing the production efficiency of modern manufacturing industries. Companies that provide services of research and development stay in the high-end position in the industrial chain, as they can increase the technology level and added value of products through research, development and innovative design to enhance core competence of high-tech industries and modern manufacturing industries for the continuous improvement in the quality and efficiency of urban economic development.

(2) The producer service industry can achieve economies of scale and improve urban economic functions. The producer service industry often agglomerate for the development to obtain economies of scale, which also optimises the spatial layout of urban industries and further improves the functions of the urban economy to provide services. In the development of modern urban economy, producer service enterprises are more likely to agglomerate for various public resources in cities to reduce costs in the production process. The resulting economies of scale and the promotion of forming the overall industrial chain are known as internal economies of scale. Since the producer service industry is a "fragmented" industry, the provision of a producer service requires the cooperation of relevant industries. As a result, a number of companies involved in the producer service industry would agglomerate in cities and form external economies of scale, which is the "urbanised economy". Regardless of the expansion of production scale and the increase in the variety of services, geographical agglomeration would help companies to obtain more factors of production at lower charges, and the fixed cost of production would decrease, because of the increasing number of products, enterprises and even industrial activities. The overall cost of the production process would gradually decrease with the agglomeration of producer service companies. Due to the excellent ability of the modern producer service industry to connect with other industries in the industrial system, it can drive the

development of various industries in cities and achieve larger economies of scale to promote the optimisation of urban industrial structure and the overall economic prosperity.

(3) The producer service industry can increase knowledge spillovers and improve urban innovation capabilities. Producer service companies mainly agglomerate in a diversified and specialised manner in the interior of cities, clusters are the important carriers for the agglomeration and development of the producer service industry. This is also an inevitable trend in the development of spatial structure in the producer service industry. More producer service companies with synergy and learning effects agglomerate in certain areas, which is conducive to knowledge spillovers and efficient innovation, so as to enhance the overall competitiveness of enterprises and cities. As the pressure of competition increases, manufacturing companies have higher demand for producer services. The upcoming knowledge spillovers accelerate the research and development of products and improve the management in manufacturing companies, and eventually promote technological innovation for more progress. Because of high proportion of knowledge and technology, the producer service industry occupies the high-end position in the industrial chain to have strong control over resources and good transformation into innovation. It has a direct and leading impact in innovation of knowledge and services, and creates conditions for urban innovation. The spread of knowledge spillovers and the formation of mechanisms for technological innovation are conducive to improving the technological level and quality of the entire industrial

system in urban areas. Therefore, modern producer service enterprises are the main carriers for the improvement of urban innovation capabilities, and they are very significant for the realisation of urban economic transformation.

(4) The producer service industry can alleviate the pressure on resources and the environment for sustainable economic development. The producer service industry strengthens the dependence of industrial development on knowledge and technology by promoting knowledge spillovers and technological innovation to reduce the large consumption of resources and energy in the earlier process of industrialisation and reduce conflicts between economic growth and the ecological system. Firstly, the producer service industry promotes the position of industrial enterprises in the industrial chain by improving the quality of the intermediate input in the production process, so as to improve the operational efficiency and core competitiveness of enterprises continuously. Secondly, the development of the producer service industry improves the use of information technology in the production process. Promoting industrialisation with the use of information technology can improve the modernisation of industrial enterprises and the acceptance, improvement and innovation of new technologies. Thirdly, the producer service industry is essentially an alternative to the material input by increasing the service input in the production process. This can change the poor management of the environment from production end in the past. It is also is conducive to the coordination between economic development and the ecological system for a new development pattern of

industrialisation with low consumption of resources and less environmental pollution. At the same time, the producer service industry plays an active role in developing the employment rate, resources, the environment, infrastructure and the comprehensive carrying capacity in urban areas, and building ecological cities. Constructing the producer service industry not only produces economic but also social benefits in the process of urban development.

Chapter 2.2 The Economic Transformation of Metropolises in Developed Countries and Their Development Pattern of the Producer Service Industry

Since the 1950s, metropolises of developed countries have faced difficulties of development and economic crises in varying degrees, such as the reduction in professional labor, capital, the employment rate and taxation, the worsening ecology and infrastructure and the increase of the number of poor people. For this, metropolises of developed countries have begun to rely on the producer service industry to adjust the industrial structure for the transformation of the economic development pattern, mainly including industrial diversification, alternative model for industrial upgrading and high-end industrial integration.

Chapter 2.2.1 New York: Industrial Diversification

Industrial diversification refers to the urban transformation of a monotonous industrial pattern in resource extraction, processing, manufacturing or traditional service industries to an industrial structure that combines advanced manufacturing, high-tech and modern producer service industries for coordinated development. New York is the largest economic centre in the United States, as well as a centre for finance, trade, culture and information exchange in the world. It ranks first in the global rankings of urban competitiveness, and it is considered to be a successful example of international metropolises. The industrial revolution started in the mid-19th century and influenced the world. Thanks to internal and external factors, such as geographical advantages as a port, technological innovation and policies, New York developed as a young city and the manufacturing industry grew rapidly to become the most important manufacturing centre, which was dominated by light industries like printing, publishing and textiles, in the United States at the end of the 19th century. After the Second World War, a large number of new industrial cities emerged risen, and the manufacturing industry in New York began to decline, so the number of jobs fell sharply. The oil crisis caused frequent economic crises in the late 1970s and early 1980s, which also further aggravated the decline of the manufacturing industry in New York, and labor productivity became worse and worse in industries. As a result, the unemployment rate in industries increased significantly. As service industries failed to absorb the unemployed population from the manufacturing industry, the overall employment rate declined in New York. A large number of manufacturing headquarters and office buildings moved out of New

York, and fiscal revenues decreased greatly. In particular, the financial crisis in 1975 almost led to the bankruptcy in the government of New York City. To cope with the crisis, New York began to switch from traditional industries to producer service industries. It was the development of the producer service industry, such as financial services and business services, that brought New York out of the predicament. In the 1980s, New York became an international centre for business, finance and corporate headquarters after a short period of development. The most advanced and complete producer service companies agglomerated there to provide producer services for the United States and even the world. As a consequence, New York transformed from a production-oriented manufacturing centre to a commercial centre to trade commodities and capital. The economy expanded once again, thus achieved the urban transformation successfully. In 2005, the ratio of output in New York's three industries was 0.2 : 11.4 : 88.4, and the output value of service industries accounted for 88.4% of the gross domestic product. According to the employment rate in three industries, the rate was 89.3% in service industries. In 2008, New York had a total of 1021 multinational companies in the modern producer service industry. If the companies were classified by the number of companies, the three pillar industries in New York should be logistics, information technology, and financial banking. The number of companies in the fields of logistics and information technology accounted for 39.76% of the total number of multinational companies in the modern producer service industry. It should be noted that from the 1970s to 2000, New

York was at the top of international cities, and the agglomeration rate of producer services was as high as 90%. As a large number of emerging cities started to increase competition between cities, the degree of agglomeration in the producer service industry showed a downward trend with obvious decentralisation in New York after 2000. However, the decline of traditional manufacturing in New York did not mean that the manufacturing industry vanished. In fact, New York's clothing, printing, cosmetics and other industries rank the first in all cities in the United States. Machine manufacturing, military production, petroleum processing and food processing also play an important role. Currently, New York is the third largest industrial centre in the United States after Chicago and Los Angeles. Some core manufacturing industries still maintain world-class advantages on the basis of technological upgrading and high-end development.

The experience of developing the producer service industry in New York is shown below. Firstly, industrial policies are made to encourage the development of the producer service industry. New York developed a series of programs to promote industrial reorganisation in order to encourage the development of the producer service industry. The measures were mainly about increasing investment in research and development to encourage enterprises to innovate and enhance the competitiveness of traditional industries, promoting policies to support traditional industrial enterprises through government procurement, corporate financing, subsidies for research and development, so as to promote technological transformation and industrial upgrading of traditional manufacturing industries. For high-tech enterprises, the fees for renting high-end offices, using supporting facilities, transportation and communication equipment would be reduced to lower operating costs of high-tech enterprises at the early stage of development. New York also implemented the strategies of digitalisation with the use of information technology to connect with the world through the Internet. This allowed New York to become the global centre of various services and the advanced producer service industry. These useful policies enabled the financial, insurance, accounting, consulting, information and other producer services to grow rapidly in New York. Secondly, New York strengthened the dominant position of the producer service industry through industrial agglomeration for development. In New York, Manhattan is the centre of economic activities, where advanced producer service companies agglomerate intensively. Manhattan attaches significant importance to the creation of a good environment for enterprises by planning and guiding the development of industrial clusters in the producer service industry, such as the construction of many fully equipped commercial office buildings, conference and exhibition centres as well as residential apartments. New York intensively developed rail transit like subway to facilitate the transportation of people in the central area, ease the pressure of urban traffic, and encourage professional workers of the producer service industry to work and start businesses in Manhattan. The government of New York City also made an active, scientific municipal plan to create good external conditions for the agglomeration of the producer service industry. Thirdly, New York trained a large number of professional talents for the development of producer service companies. New York has always focused on education. More than 20% of its annual expenditure is spent on education every year. Through implementing a series of vocational training programs, New York improved the education level of the labor force and provided a large number of high-quality professionals for the development of the producer service industry to meet the requirements of constructing a service economy. New York can also benefit from numerous universities, scientific research institutions, and enterprises that locate there. Based on the demand, the government developed policies of education and training for the needs of scientific and technological progress and economic development. The highly educated and professional workforce can create high productivity efficiently for quick industrial transformation of New York from traditional services to modern producer services.

Chapter 2. 2. 2 London: Alternative Model for Industrial Upgrading

The alternative model for industrial upgrading refers to the replacement of traditional industries by urban high-tech industries and the replacement of low value-added industries by high value-added industries, which would be the most complete pattern for industrial transformation. London's industrial transformation from a "global factory" to a "creative city" is a typical example of how the alternative model works for industrial upgrading successfully. London is the birthplace of the industrial revolution and modern capitalism. It is also one of the centres of international finance, logistics and information, and the largest capital market in the European Union. After 1760, the British industrial revolution led to an unprecedented growth in London's manufacturing industry with the focus on traditional industries, such as textiles, steel, and heavy machinery. They became "the sunset industries" quickly in the 1950s, the population of industrial employees fell sharply, and many industrial enterprises faced the risk of shutdown. In order to overcome the dilemma of industrial development, London began to intensively develop the financial industry for the replacement in the late 1970s and early 1980s, and quickly became one of the three major financial centres in the world, other than New York and Zurich. London has the world's largest market for international insurance, over-the-counter derivatives, lending business, and gold with the highest liquidity. In 2003, London's financial services and added value accounted for 42% of the total proportion in the country. 16.8% of the gross domestic product in London was attributed to the financial service industry with more than 300000 employees. After 20 years of development, the growth of London's financial service industry slowed down gradually. London had to start a new round of economic reorganisation, and the development of creative industries brought new opportunities for urban construction. Through the generation, protection and access of intellectual property, creative industries are based on the activities of individual creativity, skills and talents to give full play to the effectiveness of creating wealth and employment by knowledge.

Creative industries are not only the results of developing new technologies rapidly, but also the combination of new technologies and those ideas relating to intellectual property with traditional industries, reflecting a new development trend of modern industries. At the same time, the industry of start-up businesses would be also a typical energy-saving industry, which would reduce the dependence of cities on energy and improve the urban ecosystem. The environment of the Thames in London was also improved thoroughly during this period to provide a sustainable path for the development of industries. At present, the contribution of 13 creative industries-such as advertising, architecture, design, publishing, software and computer services-to the economy in London has surpassed the financial service industry and completely changed the business model in the past. London is no longer a city that concentrates on production and manufacturing but new concepts of creativity and marketing to plan for urban development. In this old industrialised city, London's manufacturing industry had made brilliant achievements, but it had lost its competitiveness completely under the new round of technological revolution. With the development of creative industries, London completed the transformation of industrial structure, realised the transformation of urban economy successfully for the new economic vitality.

The successful transformation of London is mainly based on the following important measures. Firstly, the government planed and guided innovation actively. In 2000, the London Development Agency took the lead to formulate the "Strategic Plan for Science, Knowledge and

Innovation in London" under the cooperation between 15 government departments and 10 non-governmental associations, leading to a trend of making innovations in science and education. In 2003, the "London Development Agency" announced "the Action Plan for Innovation Strategies in London (2003—2006)", which analysed advantages and disadvantages of innovation in London companies thoroughly and made preconditions and recommendation of policies for industrial transformation. Secondly, London combined research and promotion of policies. To ensure the scientific and consistent policies for creative industries, the United Kingdom has began to develop creative industries on the national level, and listed the development of creative industries as an important policy for national industries since 1997. The government defined 13 creative industries, guided them to agglomerate and provided an exchange platform for venture capital and workers in creative industries. Thirdly, London created good conditions for the development of small and medium-sized enterprises. In the process of constructing creative industries, small and medium-sized enterprises are the mainstay of development, and London also gave great policies to support them. In order to encourage small and medium-sized enterprises to develop new products independently, London launched the "Policies of Tax Reduction and Exemption for Investment in Research and Development" in 2000 to encourage enterprises to invest in research and development. To solve the financing problems of small and medium-sized enterprises, London launched the "Plan for Loan Guarantee of Small Enterprises" and the "Plan for Loan in Training Programs of

Small Enterprises" in 2003 to reduce the financing costs. These measures achieved remarkable results in promoting the development of central enterprises in creative industries.

Chapter 2.2.3 Tokyo: High-End Industrial Integration

High-end strategies of industries are to realise the industrial transformation and functional upgrading of cities through the development of high-end industries in the value chain, such as high-tech industries, and modern service industries. This also includes the related research and development of industries, marketing as well as other high-end activities in the value chain. Tokyo completed the urban transformation from a typical "manufacturing centre" to a "centre of headquarters". Currently, Tokyo is the city with the largest number of Fortune 500 companies (there were 51 companies in 2010) and becomes a successful example of urban transformation through developing high-end parts in industries. In the Second World War, the Japanese economy was greatly affected. For the quick economic recovery, the Japanese government implemented strategies to prioritise the development of the heavy chemical industry. As the centre of the Japanese economy, Tokyo rapidly formed an industrial structure dominated by the heavy chemical industry. After the mid-1960s, with the rapid growth of the Japanese economy, the proportion of the output value and the employment rate in service industries began to rise. Tokyo started to develop in the phase of post-industrialisation, and the industrial structure also tended to be optimised. Even though the industry was still the leading industry in Tokyo, the proportion began to decline gradually. In the 1970s, there were tremendous changes in the external environment of Japan ' s economic development. More specifically, energy crisis, environmental pollution, appreciation of Japanese currency, and rising costs of domestic production affected the direction of Tokyo ' s industrial development and its internal structure directly. This reconstructed the pattern of economic development which was jointly promoted by the secondary and tertiary industries in the past. In 1970, Tokyo ' s service industries accounted for 67.9% of the gross domestic product, and the producer service industry became the main driving force for economic development gradually. At the same time, the technological advancement brought by the development of the producer service industry allowed the strategic transformation of electrical and transportation machinery in Japan to high value-added production methods. It countered the adverse effects brought by the appreciation of Japanese currency and showed stronger competitiveness than before, making it a leading industry in Japan and greatly reducing the impacts of the Japan-US agreement on the decline in the proportion of the Japanese manufacturing industry in the industrial structure. Tokyo ' s advanced manufacturing industies including automobile manufacturing, household appliances, precision instruments, petroleum refining, printing and publishing, production of pharmaceutical preparation, and manufacturing of electronic components, receive strong support from the producer service industry. Manufacturing companies in Tokyo still rank first in terms of quantity and competitiveness nationwide, and they also stay in a leading position in the world.

Tokyo's measures of developing the producer service industry are the effective organisation of all the industrial policies, which mainly include the following aspects. Firstly, Tokyo developed industrial policies to promote the integrated development of manufacturing and producer service industries. Under the organic coordination between the production and living conditions, Tokyo with the Ota Machinery Industrial Cluster retained as the manufacturing industrial center and developed it into the centre of Japanese machinery industries with the characteristic of innovation. The high-end development of the manufacturing industry drove the development of the producer service industry, as the added value of its products mainly came from the producer service industry. Because of the increasing competition in the market, manufacturing companies started to outsource their non-core businesses gradually in order to maintain the core competence and make better use of the specialised division of labor. Relying on more professional and functional producer service enterprises to integrate their own superior resources promoted the development of the producer service industry greatly. Secondly, Tokyo focused on economic transformation to optimise the industrial division of labor in various regions of the city. In the core area, Tokyo focused on the development of producer services, such as commerce, finance and insurance, and publishing and printing. In the peripheral area, Tokyo developed advanced manufacturing industries, such as heavy machinery and precision instruments. In this way, optimising the industrial layout of the core area and the peripheral area can give full play to the coordination and organisation of Tokyo's urban economic system. Thirdly, Tokyo benefited from technological innovation completely. Innovation promoted the development of new products, technologies and emerging service industries, and increased the technological level of the producer service industry to encourage other industries to make more innovations. Tokyo's five emerging fields in the producer service industry, such as information, industrial design, and business management and consulting, provided direct services for other industries and continued to promote the development of service industries and other industries. Fourthly, Tokyo promoted the reform of privatisation in monopolistic industries and the development of the producer service industry. In order to meet the advent of the information age, the Japanese government began to reduce the market access barriers of the producer service industry in the 1980s and reduced the control over prices. Privatisation was promoted in the monopolistic fields of producer services, such as transportation, communication operations, electric power and financial insurance, so as to enhance the competitiveness of the entire industry and promote enterprises to improve business management and operational efficiency. Since the 1990s, the Japanese government further promoted the reform of the market access barriers, so the access to the markets were expanded into different industries gradually. At present, Japan's institutional reform involves most economic and social fields. The reform has promoted the economic and social changes in Tokyo, and it is a necessary prerequisite for promoting the effective development of the producer service industry.

Chapter 2.3 The Economic Transformation of China's Metropolises and Development Patterns of the Producer Service Industry

Due to the international financial crisis in 2008, China's long-term export-oriented strategies was shattered to a great extent. In globalisation, the role of being a "manufacturing country" has experienced significant changes, and it is extremely urgent to transform the pattern of economic development. As a result, China faces the pressure of transforming the economic development pattern from exogenous to endogenous. In urban areas, it is also urgent to promote transformation and development, as China's cities are entering the important stage of transformation and development. As prices of urban land and labor have increased and environmental protection has become stricter in developed regions, the development strategy is challenged that relies on labor-intensive industries as the mainbody for overseas markets, due to the global economic recession. Intensively developing advanced manufacturing and modern producer service industries has become the target in most cases of urban economic transformation. Key factors that influence the success of urban transformation would be whether cities can change the extensive development pattern, overcome the conflicts between resources and the environment, the uncoordinated economic development of internal and external resources, and the lack of independent innovation (Gu, 2011).[53] As the most developed cities in China and the central cities in the region of Beijing-Tianjin-Hebei and the Yangtze River Delta respectively, Beijing and Shanghai have made brave attempts to develop the producer service industry. They achieved remarkable results, and the advantages of urban competitiveness were further improved, which also created conditions for a rational division of labor between cities.

Chapter 2.3.1 Beijing: High-End Service Industries with Comprehensive Functions and Well-Planned Layout

At the early stage after the founding of the People's Republic of China, Beijing was not only a political center but also a large industrial city. In accordance with the requirements of "Beijing's First Urban Planning (1953)", Beijing built a number of manufacturing enterprises focusing on textiles machinery, building materials and other light industries outside Jianguomen, and formed the industrial zone in the eastern suburb. Since then, the idea of building Beijing into a centre for modern industries and technological development was further proposed in the revision of "Beijing Urban Planning (the Preliminary Urban Planning for Beijing)". From the 1950s to the 1980s, Beijing attached high importance to heavy industries, and the investment in this area accounted for more than 90% of the total industrial investment between 1958 and 1975. After the reform and opening up, industrial development seriously damaged the ecological system in Beijing, resulting in the reorganisation of urban functions. In 1982, "the Overall Planning for Urban Construction in Beijing" clarified that Beijing would function as a "centre for China's politics and culture" and began to control the scale of industrial construction strictly. A number of industrial enterprises with heavy pollution and low efficiency in the inner area were shut down, merged and restructured. During the 1990s, the development of foreign-funded enterprises in China has seriously affected the development of state-owned industrial enterprises. Local companies in machinery, food, printing, light industry and other fields suffered serious profit losses, while the environmental pollution caused by industries like metallurgy, chemical industry and building materials became increasingly serious. The Capital Steel Industrial Group also moved to Caofeidian, and traditional industries began to decline. At the end of 1992, Beijing finished the formulation of the "Overall Urban Planning for Beijing (1991—2010)", aiming at the rapid development of the tertiary industry. In particular, it is emphasised that Beijing should develop the tertiary industry intensively and establish a system of tertiary industry that helps the capital, the whole country and the world with complete functions, reasonable layout, and first-class services. After nearly 20 years of development, Beijing's industrial reorganisation achieved remarkable results. Beijing made great efforts to become a service centre for localisation in the manufacturing industry. There was rapid development in its advanced service industry, such as modern financial services, professional services (consulting, accounting, law, etc.), exhibitions and institutional services, research, development and technical services, education and training, healthcare, and cultural communication (including sports). In 2009, Beijing officially proposed the idea of building an international city, which played a very important role in promoting the rapid development of the local producer service industry. In 2013, 48 enterprises listed in the Fortune 500 established headquarters in Beijing, which surpassed Tokyo for the first time and ranked first in the world. Among the top 500 Chinese companies, 97 of them also set up headquarters in Beijing. In 2013, there were 3937 headquarters and affiliated branches in Beijing. With regard to the type of headquarters, there were 366 financial headquarters, 563 headquarters of management, 339 headquarters of research and development, and 750 marketing headquarters. They were mainly producer service enterprises or those undertaking the function of providing producer services in the development of companies. At present, Beijing's producer service industry will become the leading industrial sector of urban economy, and it will play a vital role in the region of Beijing-Tianjin-Hebei, the Bohai Sea Economic Zone and even the East Asian Economic Zone through the combination of modern manufacturing industries. The urban spatial structure that includes "networked and multiple centres, functional areas and key channels" in Beijing has gradually been demonstrated to the world.

At the macro level, the external influences from the government and market play a key role in guiding and regulating the formation of regional structure in the producer service industry. The government planning and construction could guide the market to a certain extent. The spatial distribution of the producer service industry in Beijing showed significant industrial agglomeration.The central urban area is a mixed development zone for multiple types of producer services with low homogeneity, such as financial insurance, research and development, design and engineering consulting. In the suburb, four zones were formed in terms of region and function with strong homogeneity,such as information consulting and technology services.In addition to a few cases , most of traditional state-owned producer service companies locate in the vast areas covering from the border between the suburb and the outer suburb to the outer suburb. In particular, traditional financial services and technical services are mainly to meet the basic needs of local economic development(Zhao & Zhou,2007).[54] The formation of the regional structure in Beijing's producer service industry is the result of the joint influence from the government and market during the economic transformation, and it is the process of interaction and mutual promotion between authorities and companies (Zhao et al., 2009).[55] Beijing preliminarily formed a relatively complete functional system of service industries with its advantages in politics, human resources and scientific research, the layout has become more and more reasonable. However, there are still significant gaps in the level of industrial development, compared with other international cities, such as New York and London. The role of market mechanisms in the development of the producer service industry needs to be further strengthened.

Chapter 2.3.2 Shanghai: "Dual Driving Force" of the Modern Service Industry and Advanced Manufacturing Industry

From the 1920s to the 1930s, Shanghai already had a large-scaled system of service industries with complete functions and various categories. The most typical of these was the Bund, which gathered hundreds of foreign, Chinese, and private banks, insurance companies, exchanges of stocks and other commodities. Before 1949, Shanghai was once the largest financial centre in the Far East. The financial markets of stocks, gold and foreign currency all ranked first in Asia. After the founding of the People's Republic of China, Shanghai still maintained developed service industries. However, since the implementation of the first five-year plan in 1953, Shanghai has over emphasised the secondary industry in the economic development, and the consumption and services of the city have been weakened for the following 30 years. By the end of the 1970s, Shanghai became the largest comprehensive industrial base and the economic centre of "producer services" in China. After the reform and opening up, Shanghai began to adjust the industrial structure in order to give full play to comprehensive urban functions. The reform of the economic system, especially the major strategic decision to "build Shanghai as one of the centres for international economy, finance and trade rapidly with the development and opening up of Pudong as the leading part" promoted Shanghai to the forefront of reform and opening up as well as national economic development. This put Shanghai's economic development to a period of good and normal development, and the industrial structure was also changed correspondingly. In 1999, the total output value of Shanghai's service industries exceeded RMB 200 billion for the first time, which surpassed the secondary sector and accounted for 50% of the city's gross domestic product. In 2009, the proportion of Shanghai's service industries reached 59.4%, and the producer service industry accounted for 38.2%. In order to give full play to its comparative advantages, Shanghai adopted a development pattern of "dual driving force" that "prioritises the development of modern service industry and advanced manufacturing industry", and the modern service industry is mainly based on the knowledge-intensive and technology-intensive producer service industry. At present, Shanghai functions as the centre of the producer service industry to complete outsourced tasks of delivering international advanced producer services. On the other hand, as the economic base of headquarters, Shanghai can provide important support for the manufacturing industry in the Yangtze River Delta region. The Yangtze River Delta is China's largest manufacturing base, forming a modern urban division of labor system based on the main role played by Shanghai. Due to the rapid development of the producer service industry, Shanghai's gross domestic product per capita exceeded US $ 10000 in 2008 and reached US $ 11451 in 2009, which was equivalent to the level of the moderately developed countries or regions in the world. With the improvement of the economic level, Shanghai's producer service industry showed a trend of acceleration. In 2014, the top ten key areas of the producer service industry achieved a total operating income of more than RMB 1.8 trillion, with a year-on-year increase of 18%. The functional area in the producer service industry functioned as an important carrier for the upstream and downstream of the industrial chain, agglomeration of key industries and economic development. This area became the new driving force to promote the future industrial development in Shanghai. Shanghai relied on the development of the producer service industry, taking huge responsibility of serving China and the rest of the world and connecting the "Yangtze River Delta". Shanghai was committed to building a modern international metropolis quickly.

The industrial agglomeration of Shanghai's producer service industry mainly includes three typical development paths: primordial, embedded, and exogenous patterns, indicating the integrated development. The primordial pattern would be similar to industrial clusters in a Marshallian Industrial District, functioning with a high degree of specialisation. A large number of strongly connected small and medium-sized enterprises agglomerate in an atomic manner, with a high degree of internal mobility in industrial clusters. They share specialised labor and knowledge spillovers to form an integrated and efficient mechanism of innovation, such as the cluster of architectural design formed around the Tongji University and the cluster of engineering management formed around the Shanghai Jiaotong University. The embedded pattern would be similar to industrial clusters of satellite platforms, mainly agglomerating for branches of large enterprises. The competitiveness of industrial clusters depends on the influence of corporate headquarters, but there are fewer internal connections. The connections mainly take place between subsidiaries and headquarters, like the financial district of Lujiazui, where the world's major banks set up branches. The exogenous pattern would be similar to industrial clusters of central industries that promote the surrounding area. The connections mainly occur between core enterprises and small and medium-sized enterprises in the surrounding area. Small and medium-sized enterprises provide support for core enterprises, so the clusters are highly professional. The division of labor mainly focuses on the division of the value chain in core enterprises, such as the bonded area of Waigaoqiao. The government of Shanghai has different policies for the agglomeration in various industries. For the agglomeration of primordial producer services, the government mainly provides guidance of policies, technical subsidies, financing benefits and so on. For the agglomeration of embedded producer services, the government mainly provides infrastructure support, strengthens industrial supervision, and regulates industrial development for more manufacturing companies. For the agglomeration of exogenous producer services, the government mainly supports the development of core enterprises or introduces advanced service enterprises directly from other countries, and makes it develop rapidly to give full play to the leading role of those enterprises in economic growth (Gao, 2008).[56]

Chapter 2. 4 Comparative Analyses of the Development of the Producer Service Industry in Domestic and Foreign Cities

Through comparative analyses, it is found that there are significant differences in development paths, although the trend of transforming the urban economy and constructing the producer service industry is consistent. Only those cities with good conditions can become a centre for the producer service industry, stay at the high end of the global value chain and enhance the sustainable development of urban economy. These conditions include economic globalisation and the development of information technology to provide possibilities for upgrading the development of the producer service industry through outsourcing services. At the same time, the degree of economic development and industrialisation needs to create demand for the producer service industry. Industrial agglomeration is an important driving force for the development of the producer service industry. The necessary preconditions for the development of the producer service industry also include a good institutional environment, complete infrastructure, friendly policies, and sufficient professional labor.

Chapter 2.4.1 The Background of Urban Economic Transformation and Development of the Producer Service Industry

The transformation of the service economy of cities is normally carried out after a country has gradually entered the post-industrial stage under the background of economic globalisation with the promotion of information technology. It is a very important feature that can be seen as a process. During the process of economic transformation in developed countries, there are not only global international metropolises, such as New York, London and Tokyoy. Instead, almost all cities have experienced the trend of reorganising the economic structure in the adjustment of the globalised division of labor. After the 1990s, developed economies have stepped into the post-industrial society. On as one hand, the trend of globalisation has brought a new round of international industrial transformation, and the vertical international division of labor has become increasingly apparent. The manufacturing industries in developed countries shifted to developing countries for relatively cheap land and labor. They use monopolies of knowledge and advantages of capital to focus on the production and supply of capital-intensive, technology-intensive and producer services to control the high end of the industrial chain and lead the global economy. A large number of developing countries are mainly engaged in the processing industry with medium and high intensity of labor, heavy consumption of resources and low level of technology. Developing countries are stuck at the low end of the value chain, and they gradually become processing and manufacturing factories for developed countries. On the other hand, the popularisation and application of information technology has caused a technological revolution in related industries and accelerated the transformation and upgrading of traditional industries. Information technology has been widely used in automotive industry, machinery manufacturing, aerospace, new materials and other industries through CAD, CAM, CIMS, computing simulation and other systematic technologies, greatly reducing costs and time taken by research and development. Metropolitan cities in developed countries, such as New York, London and Tokyo, have adapted to the trend of economic development. They transformed the economy successfully and continued to be the centre of the global economy. Globalisation and the development of information technology have strengthened competence of metropolises in developed countries and accelerated the development of international trade in services, providing an opportunity for urban development in developing countries. In the process of outsourcing and providing international services, the headquarters of multinational corporations gathered in international cities, such as New York, London and Tokyo, would provide knowledge spillovers to the supporting enterprises or subsidiaries in developing countries through the exchange of talents, information and capital. Therefore, under the premise of safeguarding national security, we should actively provide international services. For the central cities of developing countries, such as Beijing and Shanghai, they should benefit from their advantageous position, especially to meet the huge demand in the interior. Developing producer services for outsourcing business is an effective way to transform and upgrade the industrial and economic structure. This would lead to the economic transformation in the entire country to change the way of economic development (Yuan & Shi, 2008).[57]

Chapter 2.4.2 The Integration of Urban Manufacturing Industry and the Producer Service Industry for Development

As the structure of the manufacturing industry in developed countries is accelerating the transformation to the technology-intensive and high-tech one, and the low-end manufacturing technology would be moved to developing countries quickly. the urban economic structure of developed countries shows a trend of "hollowing out" and "lightening". In order to achieve economic transformation, New York and London have experienced a process of "de-industrialisation". However, there is a lag of development in the growth of the producer service industry to offset the decline in manufacturing. It took about 20 years to return to the level before the transformation. Although Tokyo has always been Japan's largest manufacturing centre, there was also a certain degree of decline in the manufacturing industry during the transformation. The growth of the producer service industry was higher than the decline in the manufacturing industry, so the number of employees in Tokyo kept increasing during that period. The position of the manufacturing industry is declining, but developed countries still master the core technologies of traditional industries, especially in multinational corporations gathered in metropolises, and gain profits by continuously transferring the non-core technological patents to developing countries. At the same time, multinational companies establish branches in some well-developed countries or regions to integrate local resources and accelerate the integration of manufacturing and producer service industries, so as to provide a larger market for its development and promote the development of "providing services of manufacturing" or "service-oriented manufacturing". For Beijing and Shanghai, the investment in the producer service industry has a positive correlation with the improvement of efficiency in the manufacturing industry, but the effect is not outstanding. This is mainly because cities with the developed producer service industry form a complete industrial chain around manufacturing and production to provide producer services for various requirements in the production process. Due to China's extensive economic development pattern, the manufacturing industry is at the low end of the value chain and unable to form effective demand for the producer service industry. Therefore, we need to work hard to extend the industrial chain of the producer service industry and promote the specialised division of labor to improve the comprehensive competitiveness of the producer service industry and accelerate the urban transformation from a manufacturing city to a service-centred city.

Chapter 2.4.3 The Spatial Reconstruction of Urban Industries and the Development of the Producer Service Industry

At the early stage of metropolitan development, the formation of industrial structure is often based on the use of resources, labor, land, location and other comparative advantages to develop related manufacturing industries. Through continuous agglomeration of factors, industrial clusters are formed to obtain external economies, such as knowledge spillovers, economies of scale, markets of specialised labor and industrial linkages, making it a centre for the manufacturing industry and the industrial economy. When the environment, land and public facilities cannot afford, the manufacturing industry that greatly depends on factors of production will move to the interior and even outside metropolises with lower costs of land and labor. In the process of distributing manufacturing companies to the outside of cities, the producer service industry is gradually separated from the manufacturing enterprises by doing business in "outsourcing services", becoming an independent organisation of producer services and promoting the further development of the metropolitan economy. In order to maintain competitiveness, some manufacturing companies outsource non-strategic activities with less added value in the production process through "outsourcing production" or "providing services of manufacturing" to realise the transformation from a manufacturing enterprise to a producer service enterprise. Metropolises would gradually develop into an industrial structure based on the agglomeration of service economy. Through technology, intellectual capital, human resources and other advanced factors of production by the producer service enterprises that agglomerate in central areas, production would be more roundabout and specialised with more investment of capital to promote industrial reorganisation effectively. Through the spatial distribution of division of labor, the producer service industry provides services for the interior in large cities and even the manufacturing industry outside the large cities. This is to further improve the efficiency in the manufacturing industry and promote the expansion of market to enhance the economic influencing power of large cities in the surrounding area. Compared with the manufacturing industry, the producer service industry is difficult to standardise, as it is more dependent on human resources, knowledge and technology. Therefore, developing the producer service industry can become a more stable and long-lasting source of competitiveness for cities, and it would be the mainstream of industrial development in urban areas inevitably. The producer service industry forms a "centralised layout" in the economic centre of cities. That is to say, the producer service industry is agglomerated in cities, but companies are categorised by specialised division of labor to distribute in different regions, so both of industrial agglomeration and separate distribution can exist at the same time. Trading activities that involve uncomplicated and standardised services tend to be separate in spatial layout, while those involving complex and customised services tend to agglomerate. The central area is still a centre for high-end services, such as finance, law, advertising, consulting and management. Traditional central business districts cannot withstand the high intensity of economic development, thus forming the new central business districts, such as Kangnam and Youngdungpo in Seoul, South Korea, Shinjuku and Shibuya in Tokyo, Japan, Lujiazui in Shanghai, Dokland in London, the United Kingdom, and La Défense in Paris, France. They play some of the functions of traditional central business districts and gather high-end producer service companies and corporate headquarters. Some corporate headquarters and office activities in the producer service industry, such as data processing, logistics, research and development, design, engineering services, are starting to be moved to the suburbs. In the process of sustainable urban development, the capabilities of agglomerating and distributing the producer service industry are promoted mutually for the orderly and rational spatial layout of urban industries. As a result, the urban industrial reorganisation would be completed and the functions as a metropolitan economic centre would be strengthened continuously in the regional economy.

Chapter 2. 4. 4 The Market Improvement and Development of the Producer Service Industry with Government Supports

The rise of the producer service industry is the spontaneous process of economic reorganisation under market economy, and the free market is the fundamental driving force. As the most important centre of the producer service industry, the urban traffic accessibility, prices and rental fees of land, labor market, supporting facilities, reputation of geographical location are very significant. What's more, the government's active guidance and preferential policies for industrial development also play a decisive role. At the macro level, the external influences from the government and the market play a key role in guiding and regulating the formation of regional structure in the producer service industry. The government planning and construction could guide the market to a certain extent. The key role successfully played by the producer service industry in New York, London and Tokyo in the economic transformation is related to the stagnant urban economic development and the decline of the manufacturing industry. On the other hand, it is also linked to the proper introduction of various effective policies by the city government. The implementation of such policies is more like indirect intervention with the use of market mechanisms, such as improving infrastructure, encouraging technological innovation, building financing platforms, and developing professional education. China's urban development is mostly led by the government, and the government has absolute control and decision-making power over resources and regional agglomeration. Therefore, the essence of China's urban economic growth is that cities have excessive dependence on capital and land. Due to excessive dependence on investment, a large amount of capital is wasted in the fields with overcapacity, resulting in a continuous decline in capital productivity. At the same time, it also weakens the ability to absorb labor in economic growth, which restricts the national economic growth quickly. In areas with rapid economic development, the expansion of urban land use is also relatively fast, but the efficiency of using urban land is not high in China. The expansion of constructed area in cities is obviously faster than the growth of non-agricultural population in cities, indicating that capacity of gathering population is weak and the land and resources are wasted. In the process of urban development, appropriate government intervention can control the negative externalities and optimise the allocation of resources in the case of market failure. However, if the government intervenes too much, it would result in the lack of market mechanisms and lead to the distorted economic development. At present, the fundamental problem in China's urban development lies in the excessive direct intervention in the market economy. The prediction of industrial development is insufficient, and the excessive government intervention caused by the unreasonable evaluation system of performances hinders the functions of the market. Urban development is ultimately to achieve coordinated development of the environment, economy and society. The city government needs to learn to be a regulator and guide for urban development, understand the nature, functional orientation and development goals scientifically. The government should really take into account the quality, taste and living standards of the city to create the necessary conditions for the sustainable development of urban economy.

Chapter Three

Measurements of Total Factor Productivity in the Producer Service Industry and Regional Differences

In 2014, China's gross domestic product was RMB 636.463 billion, marking the milestone of more than RMB 60 trillion. The added value of the tertiary industry was RMB 306.73 billion and accounted for 48.2% of the gross domestic product, which was 5.6% higher than that of the secondary industry. The greater proportion of the tertiary industry indicated that China officially entered the era of the "service-oriented" economy, implying that the Chinese economy shifted from industry-led to service-oriented. Service industries would become the new driving force for China's economic growth under the new normal. Service industries play an increasingly important role in economic development. More than 70% of the employment rate and output is contributed by the service industry in developed countries. However, the growth of productivity in service industries has always been slow, and people used to consider that the development of service industries was backward. This seems to be wired in the process of economic growth. Although service industries grow slowly in production efficiency, there is no doubt that the proportion of service industries in the total output value and the employment rate keeps rising gradually. Therefore, it is necessary to make a reasonable distinction within service industries and measure the productivity of factors of production scientifically in order to accurately understand service industries, especially the key role played by the producer service industry in economic growth.

Chapter 3.1 Baumol's Cost Disease in Service Industries and Total Factor Productivity

In 1967, Baumol proposed the famous theory of "cost disease" in service industries. According to this theory, the growth rate of productivity in service industries is relatively low, compared to that of the manufacturing industry, causing the overall economic growth to decline, and the higher prices of service industries would increase the costs of the entire society. The increase in the proportion of the employment rate in service industries and output value in economic activities would also lead to a decline in the overall growth rate, mainly because of the lower growth rate of productivity in service industries and the impacts on total factor productivity.[58] Since then, many scholars began to examine Baumol's hypothesis. The figures of most developed countries indicate that there is a negative relationship between the proportion of service industries and the growth of the total productivity, which reflects in both production and employment (Rubalcaba, 2007).[59] Since the reform and opening up, empirical research on China's service industries also seems to indicate that the growth rate is declining with time, although the total factor productivity of service industries continues to increase in China (Yang, 2008 [60]; Hu, 2010 [61]; Liu & Zhang, 2010 [62]). Therefore, the growth of labor productivity of China's service industries is also considered to be underdeveloped (Cheng, 2004).[63] However, it should be pointed out that, unlike output of the manufacturing industry, it is difficult to calculate service industries accurately and often it is underestimated by people, which would affect the accurate measurement of labor productivity in service industries to a large extent (Gouyette & Perelman, 1997 [64]; Yue & Zhang, 2002 [65]; Jiang and Li, 2004 [66]). The rise in the price index also leads to overestimation of the increase in prices of services, which can also result in underestimation of real output and labor productivity in service industries (Bonatti & Felice, 2007).[67] More importantly, Baumol's hypothesis mainly works for end-of-use, and it is difficult to apply to those for the intermediate input. With the rise of the modern service industry, especially the development of the producer service industry, many people start to question the theory of "cost disease".

In the process of rapid economic development in China, the producer service industry provides knowledge-intensive and technology-intensive services for production of enterprises and plays an increasingly important role in economic operations. The level of productivity not only plays a decisive role in the added value of service industries, but also has important impacts on the improvement of efficiency and the increasingly specialised division of labor in the manufacturing industry. However, most of the existing studies focus on measuring the total factor productivity of service industries as a whole, which lacks in-depth and systematic analysis of the total factor productivity in the producer service industry. With the use of the data between provinces from 2004 to 2009, this book measures the total factor productivity of the producer service industry by the Cobb-Douglas production function and conducts a comparative analysis of imbalanced development between regions.

In the theoretical framework of neoclassical economic growth, the improvement of total factor productivity (TFP) is an important source of economic growth for the long term. When factors are inputted to a certain extent, the level of total factor productivity will determine the speed of economic growth. Therefore, the measurement and empirical analysis of total factor productivity has become an important part of studying modern economic growth. In the past, the measurement of total factor productivity was mainly based on the whole economy, the fields of industry or manufacturing. One of the reasons is that the development of industry or manufacturing is the main booster of economic growth in the process of industrialisation. The other reason is that the heterogeneity of service industries and the complexity of output in these industries measurement would also lead to a lower figure of total factor productivity measured in service industries. However, as developed countries enter the post-industrial era, there has been a trend of transforming the "industrial economy" to the "service-oriented economy". The development of service industries becomes an important factor in promoting economic growth, absorbing labor and enhancing industrial competitiveness, resulting in more and more attention to the measurement of total factor productivity in service industries (Rubalcaba, 2007).[59]

As the role of service industries in China's economic growth has become increasingly prominent, many scholars have begun to pay attention to the changes of total factor productivity in service industries and carried out calculations. Kesha Guo (1992) made a comparative study on the trend of the growth rate in three industries and the factors since the reform and opening up, and used the Solow residual method to calculate the average annual growth rate of total factor productivity and concluded it was 2.58% in China's service industries from 1979 to 1990.[68] Dazhong Cheng (2003) measured the growth rate of labor productivity in China's service industries according to the growth rate of output value per capita and found that it was underdeveloped. Cheng also estimated the growth rate of total factor productivity in China's service industries from 1978 to 2000 by using the total production function with the same returns to scale and found that the technological progress in China's service industries was not labor-enhanced, but slightly capital-enhanced.[69] Naihua Gu (2008) used data envelopment analysis (SFA) to explore the characteristics of how the total factor productivity grew in China's service industries from 1992 to 2002. Gu believed that the technological development was inefficient in China's service industries, and the driving force for the growth of service industries was mainly based on factors inputted, with obvious features of the extensive development.[70] Qingqing Yang et al. (2008) also used the stochastic frontier analysis to draw similar conclusions with Gu.[71] Yong Yang (2008) used the Cobb-Douglas production function to calculate the total factor productivity in China's service industries from 1952 to 2006. The research results showed that the contribution made by the growth rate of China's total factor productivity to output in service industries fluctuated greatly before 1980. After 1980, it became stable gradually, but the overall level was low. The development of service industries based on factor-driven was not compatible with low incomes earned by residents.[60] Xingkai Liu and Cheng Zhang (2010) used the non-parametric Malmquist index to measure how the total factor productivity of service industries changed in 28 Chinese provinces, districts and cities from 1978 to 2007. They pointed out that although the total factor productivity of service industries was continuously improved since the reform and opening up, the growth rate showed a trend of decline.[62]

Although the studies above were conducted with different methods, they all came to a consensus. Since the reform and opening up, the growth of China's service industries has mainly been the result of increased factor inputs, while the growth of total factor productivity shows a trend of decline, which supports Baumol's hypothesis. However, with the rise of the "service economy", the internal structure of service industries experiences significant changes. In particular, the rapid development of the producer service industry profoundly affectes the structural adjustment of the national economy while strengthening the heterogeneity in internal structure of service industries. What's more, the distinction between producer services and consumer services can be seen as a relationship between a developed economic sector and an underdeveloped economic sector. Structural inflation caused by rising wages would also reduce the total factor productivity of service industries. Therefore, the rapid growth of the producer service industry may lead to inconsistencies in the trend of how total factor productivity changes with service industries, and it is necessary to make reasonable measurements.

Chapter 3.2 Methodologies

Chapter 3.2.1 the Cobb-Douglas Production Function Model

According to the industrial characteristics of the producer service industry, this book uses growth accounting to calculate the total factor productivity of the producer service industry and its growth rate. Based on Solow residual method, growth accounting is a relatively mature method to calculate the total factor productivity. According to the requirements of the model, we need to find a suitable production function, and then use the data samples to estimate the parameters of the production function, finally measure the total factor productivity and its growth rate based on the parameters obtained. Due to the large differences in the level of economic development in China, this book uses the Cobb-Douglas production function and fixed-effect model of data to calculate the total factor productivity of the producer service industry in order to reduce impacts of regional differences on measurement.

The Cobb - Douglas production function of China ' s producer service industry is assumed below:

$$Y_{it}=A_{it}K_{it}^{\alpha}L_{it}^{\beta} \quad (3.1)$$

i represents region, t represents time, Y , K, L and A represent output, capital, labor and total factor productivity respectively, α and β stand for output elasticity of capital and labor.

The logarithm of both sides would convert the production function into a linear model:

$$\ln Y_{it}=\ln A_{it}+\alpha \ln K_{it}+\beta \ln L_{it} \quad (3.2)$$

Under the condition that returns to scale are the same ($\alpha+\beta=1$) , *the formula is transformed into*:

$$\ln Y_{it}/L_{it}=\ln A_{it}+\alpha \ln K_{it}/L_{it} \quad (3.3)$$

Conducting regression analysis of the data can obtain the output elasticity α of capital, and calculate β according to the assumption of constant returns of scale. At this time, the formula for calculating the total factor productivity can be obtained:

$$TFP_{it}= Y_{it}/(K_{it}^{\alpha}L_{it}^{\beta}) \quad (3.4)$$

The growth rate of total factor productivity in year t is:

$$tfp_{t}=(TFP_{t}-TFP_{t-1})/TFP_{t-1} \quad (3.5)$$

Chapter 3. 2. 2 the Scope Determination and the Data Analysis

Defining the scope of the producer service industry is the basis for conducting research, but the definition of scope is not the same based on different angles in specific studies and actual practices. According to "the Outline of the 12th Five-Year Plan for National Economic and Social Development of the People's Republic of China", the book divides the producer service industry into four categories - the fields of financial services, modern logistics, high-tech services, and business services. The empirical analysis is based on the data between provinces from 2004 to 2010, and the samples include 31 provinces and cities. One of the reasons for this time span would be that the Industrial Classification for National Economic Activities was newly revised in 2002. In the case, the producer service industry can be reasonably defined without the adjustment of industrial data to ensure the consistency. On the other hand, the use of the latest statistics would be conducive to improving the accuracy of conclusions, especially to assess the impacts of the international financial crisis in 2008 on the development of China's producer services. According to the national regional development strategy, the book also divides China into four regions, namely, the eastern, central, western and northeast regions, for regional comparative analysis. At the same time, I also include and make comparative analysis of Beijing and Shanghai, which are the most developed cities in China, so as to highlight the trend of the producer service industry in developed cities.

The measurement of total factor productivity in the producer service industry mainly involves the selection of three indicators to show output, capital inputs, and labor inputs. The sources of these three indicators mainly come from "the Chinese Statistical Yearbook" and the "Third Industry Statistical Yearbook". The specific measures are as follows:

(1) The first is output of the producer service industry. This variable is measured by the added value of the producer service industry in the provinces and cities from 2004 to 2010. According to the dichotomy method, this book divides service industries into the producer service industry and the consumer service industry. Since the reform and opening up, the standards of industrial classification for national economic activities were revised three times in 1985, 1994, and 2002 respectively. According to the standards of industrial classification regulated in 2002 and the definition of scope in the "Outline of the 12th Five-Year Plan for National Economic and Social Development of the People's Republic of China", this book selects eight fields in the producer service industry: finance, transportation, warehousing and postal services, information transmission, computing services and software, scientific research, technical services and geological exploration, leasing and business services. The other sectors of service industries are classified as the consumer service industry.

(2) The second is capital investment. This variable is measured by capital stock in each province and city. However, since China does not have data on capital stock, it needs to be calculated based on data on

capital formation and annual investment in fixed assets. This book estimats through the internationally accepted perpetual stock system.

$$K_{it}=I_{it}+(1-\delta)K_{it-1} \tag{3.6}$$

K_{it} is the capital stock of province i during in year t , and K_{it-1} is the capital stock of province i during year $t-1$. I_{it} is the investment in fixed assets of province i during year t , and δ is the depreciation rate.

The capital stock during the base period is estimated to be:

$$K_{i2004}=\frac{I_{i2004}}{\delta+g_i} \tag{3.7}$$

δ is the depreciation rate, and this book uses 4% as the sample that people use commonly.[94] g_i is the average growth rate in province i from 2004 to 2010. Finally, the book uses the price index of investment in fixed assets to process the primary data and obtain findings at constant prices in 2004.

(3) The third is labor input. This variable is usually based on the number of persons employed by the tertiary industry in each province and city as an indicator of labor input. However, due to the revision of "the Industrial Classification for National Economic Activities, the China Statistical Yearbook" no longer provided data on specified fields after 2003. As the producer service industry mainly agglomerate in cities, this book uses the indicator of the urban employment rate in different industries from 2004 to 2009 according to the new standards of industrial classification.

Chapter 3.3 Empirical Analyses

Based on the data of 31 provinces and cities from 2004 to 2010, this book uses Stata12 to calculate the total factor productivity of service industries and the producer service industry in each region, and conducts comparative analyses. Since this book uses the data cross many sections within a short time, there may be a problem of heteroscedasticity. Therefore, this book uses the fixed-effect model and Robust for robustness regression of heteroscedasticity. (see Table 3.1).

Table 3.1 Estimation results of the parameters in the total factor productivity models

Variable	Coefficient	Standard deviation	Test value	P value
$\ln K_{it}/L_{it}$	0.4510929***	0.0496029	9.09	0.000
Constant term	0.2909382***	0.0795627	3.66	0.000
R^2	0.9144	R^2_{adj}	0.8971	
F test	82.7	P value in F test	0.0000	
Hausman test	8.85	P value in Hausman test	0.0000	

Note: *t* in parentheses represents "*test value*". *** indicates significant results at 1% level, ** indicates significant results at 5% level, and * indicates significant results at 10% level. The calculation was completed with the use of measurement software, stata 12.

It was estimated that the output elasticity of capital in China's producer service industry from 2004 to 2010 was 0.45, and the output elasticity of labor was 0.55, indicating that the growth of output in China's producer service industry was more dependent on the increase of labor input. From 2005 to 2008, the growth rate of total factor productivity was above 10% in China's producer service industry. Due to the impacts of the international financial crisis in 2008, the growth rate of total factor productivity declined to a low point in 2009, which was the result of a sharp drop in demand of investment. In 2010, there was a recovery rebound. The international financial crisis directly influenced the development of China's trade in services, which led to a sharp decline in outsourcing business of services. Many producer service companies had difficulty in survival, due to the lack of orders. At the same time, the international financial crisis also damaged China's manufacturing industry directly. The decline in the growth of the manufacturing industry led to a decline in demand for outsourcing services, influencing the development of the producer service industry indirectly. In comparison, the growth rate of total factor productivity in service industries only reached 11.65% in 2007, and the rate was only 3.42%, 2.09% and 1.06% in 2006, 2008 and 2010 respectively. There was even negative growth in 2005 and 2009, which reflected the development was relatively lagging behind. The total factor productivity of the producer service industry grew at an average annual rate of 9.13%, while the rate was only 2.25% in service industries, which was close to the rate of 2.58% estimated by Kesha Guo (see Table 3.2).[68] Therefore, the growth of total factor productivity in China's service industries was lagging behind, but the growth rate of total factor productivity in the producer service industry was fairly rapid. Baumol's hypothesis is applicable to service industries, but it is not applicable to the producer service industry that is used as the intermediate input.

With the promotion of industrialisation and marketisation in China and the improvement of economic openness, the role of the producer service industry as the intermediate input has become more and more important, the industrial scale has kept expanding rapidly, and the economies of scale have been increasingly prominent. The growth rate of total factor productivity in the producer service industry would remain at a relative high level.

Table 3.2 Changes in total factor productivity of the producer service industry and service industries in various regions of China from 2005 to 2010 %

	Year	2005	2006	2007	2008	2009	2010	Average
Producer service industry	China	10.2597	12.9468	13.1735	11.6085	1.3529	5.4673	9.1348
	Eastern area	26.2684	12.0576	16.8355	-4.0416	16.3776	13.4769	13.4957
	Western area	13.3894	9.7828	13.3217	21.1551	-0.8757	2.4712	9.8741
	Central area	8.9841	16.9681	6.4758	25.1242	-2.8616	7.9237	10.4357
	Northeast area	13.8067	-1.7139	8.4596	8.8122	-2.5205	1.2438	4.6813
	Beijing	39.0666	18.2135	12.8543	-15.0163	35.3992	27.2002	19.6196
	Shanghai	62.6829	11.8615	20.1022	9.7969	15.3550	18.3232	23.0203
Service industries	China	-0.1078	3.4178	11.6507	2.0928	-4.6360	1.0647	2.2470
	Eastern area	4.8135	10.0679	14.1876	2.0731	4.9470	5.7465	6.9726
	Western area	2.0485	8.0893	12.2863	10.0335	-9.9797	1.0347	3.9188
	Central area	-2.7383	4.7939	3.9350	-0.9105	-6.7816	2.3148	0.1022
	Northeast area	-1.9657	-6.7454	5.4884	-1.4998	-8.2250	-4.0784	-2.8377
	Beijing	-4.5096	20.5728	22.9577	7.9572	9.3804	10.3487	11.1179
	Shanghai	-7.1766	38.5906	17.4161	36.9687	2.5814	24.5637	18.8246

Source: Department of National Accounts, National Bureau of Statistics. China Statistical Yearbook (2011). China Statistics Press, 2012.

According to the regional division, the growth rate of total factor productivity in the producer service industry in the eastern region was the fastest,with an average annual increase of 13.50%,and the growth reached 19.62% and 23.02% in Beijing and Shanghai.This was because the level of economic development in the eastern region was relatively high,and the highly developed industries stimulated the demand for the producer service industry. In addition, some of "internal" producer services provided by enterprises began to gradually "externalise" or "outsource services" for development,further promoting the production efficiency of the producer service industry. On the other hand, the eastern region had a relatively high degree of marketisation and high density of cities. There were also many "outsourcing projects of services" from developed countries,which created favourable conditions for the agglomeration and development of the producer service industry. For developing countries,the principle that service industries can only develop rapidly at the stage of post-industrialisation is changed by outsourcig services. By "outsourcing business of services",we promoted the upgrading of all parts in the industrial chain and optimised the industrial structure. At the same time, it should be noted that the development of the producer service industry in the eastern region was more sensitive to markets,especially in international metropolises like Beijing and Shanghai. The total factor productivity in Beijing and Shanghai fell sharply in 2008, while other regions reacted relatively slower to the international financial crisis.

Due to the large-scale transfer of eastern industries to the interior, the acceleration of industrialisation drove the demand for producer services effectively. The average annual growth rate of total factor productivity in the central and western regions reached 10.44% and 9.87% respectively. The total factor productivity of the producer service industry grew the slowest in the northeast, only increasing by 4.68%. The main reason was that the state-owned enterprises in the northeast accounted for a large proportion, and many companies established and developed institutions and facilities that were not directly related to the production and operation of enterprises, resulting in the lack of effective demand for the producer service industry and promotion of externalising producer services. Compared with the producer service industry, the growth rate of total factor productivity in service industries was relatively low. The growth rate of total factor productivity in the eastern region was higher than that in other regions, and the rate was even negative in the central and northeast regions. Unlike other industries, the producer service industry is "contract-intensive" to a great extent, and the production and transactions would involve more intensive and complex contractual arrangements. When the maintenance system over contracts is weak, the industrial sector, which mainly trades in tangible goods, can find other alternative mechanisms to promote transactions. For the producer service industry that trades in intangible services, it is not easy to find an alternative mechanism. Therefore, the development of the producer service industry would inevitably depend more on the improvement of marketisation and the regulation of mechanism for market operations. The growth rate of total factor productivity is also faster in the market with high degree of marketisation.

The increase in total factor productivity showed higher labor productivity, which meant that wage level that directly reflected the level of labor productivity would increase accordingly. With regards to industries, the wage level of theproducer service industry was significantly higher than other industries, and the growth rate was also fast. The average annual growth rate of wages was 20.36%, while that of the primary industry, secondary industry and consumer service industry reached only 15.14%, 18.86% and 16.34% respectively (see Figure 3.1). With the development of the economy and the adjustment of the industrial structure, the demand for the producer service industry also greatly increased. The producer service industry is highly knowledge-intensive, lying at the two ends of the industrial chain to create more added value and resulting in higher wages. This further illustrates that the Baumol's hypothesis only applies to service industries but not to the producer service industry. At the present stage in China, both the consumer service industry and the secondary industry are labor-intensive. As improving the quality of workers is a slow and long process, the level of wage increase caused by the growth in production efficiency is relatively limited. With regards to organisations in the producer service industry, the wage level of the private sector was significantly higher than that of the public sector, and the wage level in collective organisations was even lower. The difference between annual average wage level was more than RMB 10000. This showed that enhancing marketisation had positive effects on the improvement of labor productivity in the producer service industry. The positive incentives of the market are necessary conditions for the development of the producer service industry.

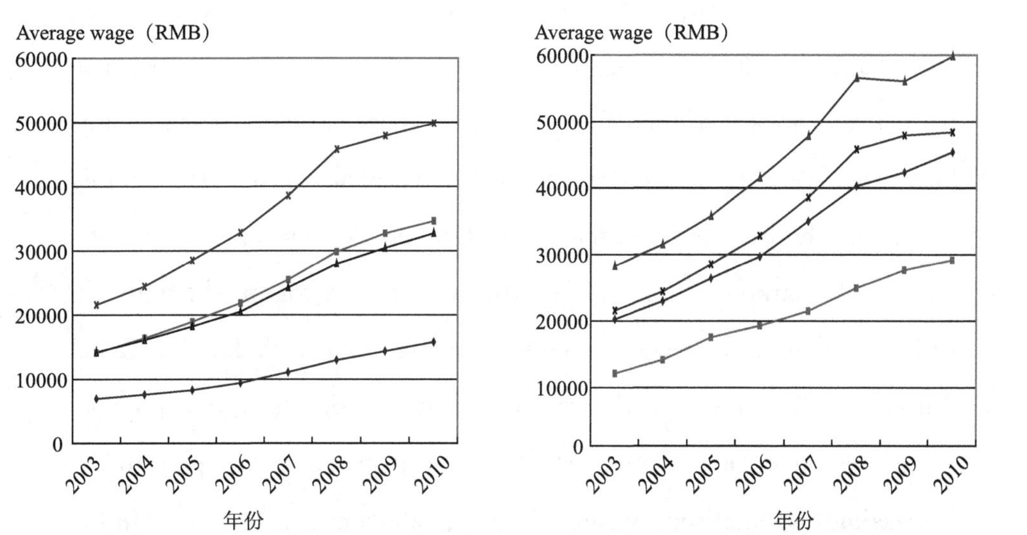

Figure 3.1 Comparison of wages between different types of organisations in the producer service industry and three industries from 2003 to 2010

Chapter 3.4 The Summary

This book uses the Cobb-Douglas production function and fixed-effect model of data to measure the growth rate of total factor productivity in China's service industries and the producer service industry from 2004 to 2010. It is found that the growth rate of total factor productivity in China's service industries was relatively lagging behind, but the rate was relatively high in the producer service industry. It also verifies that Baumol's theory "cost disease" is only applicable to service industries, but not to the producer service industry as the intermediate input.The book also compares and analyses the growth of total factor productivity in the producer services industry between regions.The growth of total factorproductivity in the eastern region was faster than that in the central and western regions, which was mainly caused by the difference in the level of economic development and the degree of marketisation. The growth of total factor productivity in China ' s producer service industry was high but with large regional differences.Therefore, a series of policies are needed to further promote the development of the producer service industry, give full play to the increasingly specialised division of labor, reduce transaction costs in the society and increase the efficiency of resource allocation through market mechanisms. First of all, it is necessary to develop the supporting policies. We should charge materials, like water, electricity, gas and land in the production, as the same price in industries, and encourage the training, development and introduction of talents in the producer service industry. Secondly, we need to gradually optimise the market environment and establish a fair, standardised and transparent market access system to break the division of sectors and industrial monopoly and develop a unified, open, competitive and orderly market for producer services.Thirdly, we should accelerate the reform of the system for services.On the one hand, we must encourage innovation in service industries, accelerate the institutional reform of state-owned enterprises, create conditions for outsourcing services and stimulate the demand for producer services. On the other hand, foreign and private capital should be encouraged to enter the field of producer services to improve the capacity of supplying producer services. Finally, it is necessary to establish a mechanism for regional cooperation to strengthen the sharing of technology, resources and knowledge in the eastern, central and western regions, and promote the coordinated development of producer services between regions. At the same time, it is necessary to promote the integration of information technology, business services and other modern producer services with the world, and promote the mutual development of regions and industries.

Chapter Four

Impacts of Developing the Producer Service Industry on Urban Industrial Transformation and Upgrading

During the period of the "11th Five-Year Plan", China's industrial added value grew at an average annual rate of 11.3%, reaching RMB 16 trillion in 2010 and accounting for 40.2% of the gross domestic product. At present, China has more than 220 types of industrial products that rank top in the world. The added value of the manufacturing industry accounts for 19.8% of the total in the world and the scale ranks first globally. No doubt that it is the global manufacturing base and the world factory (Miao, 2012).[72] However, during the period of the "12th Five-Year Plan", the internal and external environment of China's industrial development experienced profound changes. Firstly, the pattern of global economic growth was adjusted. There were negative impacts of the international financial crisis and the sovereign debt crisis, the pressure of competition from "re-industrialisation" in developed countries and the "homogeneity" in emerging economies, and rising costs of domestic capital, labor and land that constantly reduced the profit margin of China's industrial enterprises in the manufacturing process. Secondly, the popularisation of information technology promoted the integrated development of the producer service industry and industries. "Service-oriented manufacturing" reflected the new trend of advanced industrial development in the world, and it became the key to controlling the global value chain and accelerating the rise of emerging industries, such as information networks, biology and renewable energy. Thirdly, high consumption of energy and low-cost factor inputs did not increase the core competitiveness of China's industries, but it highlighted the serious conflicts, such as the lack of independent innovation for the long term and overcapacity. Therefore, accelerating industrial transformation and upgrading has been the key to transforming the economic development pattern in China. It is both the fundamental requirement for new industrialisation with Chinese characteristics, and the only way to transform from a large industrial country to a competitive industrial country.

Chapter 4.1 The Industrial Transformation and Upgrading and the Rise of the Producer Service Industry

Industrial transformation and upgrading is to promote the industrial development pattern from consuming traditional production factors to scientific and technological progress, the quality of workers and management innovation and from the extensive growth of low added value and high level of pollution to the intensive growth of high added value and low level of pollution. Through transforming traditional industries, upgrading strategic emerging industries, developing the producer service industry, and comprehensively optimising the technological structure, organisational structure, layout and industrial structure, industrial development should be truly innovation-driven, intensive, efficient and environmentally friendly to promote people's living standards and endogenous growth, and continuously enhance core competitiveness in industries and capabilities of developing the economy sustainably.[73] With the division of the global value chain and the increasingly roundabout process of production, products are also increasingly integrated into production and services. The traditional industrial development pattern that focuses on producing products is shifting to the modern industrial development pattern that provides services. Under the new changes of the development environment and competition, it is crucial to control the direction of the transformation and upgrading to "provide services" in industries for the growth of enterprises and the sustainable development of the national economy. In 2011, Apple became the listed company with the highest market value of more than US $ 500 million in the world. Its core competitiveness was not only from the sale of products. Rather, it was based on the provision of creative solutions that integrated hardware, software, digital content, and distribution channels through applications. Since the 1980s, western developed countries have stepped into the post-industrial society and began to change from the "industrial economy" to the "service economy". The producer service industry has gradually replaced industry as the main driving force for economic growth. Although the competition in the international market is about industrial products, the competitiveness of industrial products mainly comes from the investment in the producer service industry, which determines the level of industrial competitiveness of a country indirectly. The profound integration of producer services and industry becomes the most effective way to promote industrial transformation and upgrading and enhance the core competitiveness of industries.

The producer service industry provides services for producers of other goods and services as the intermediate input. It usually extends to financial services, modern logistics, high-tech services and business services. The producer service industry provides knowledge-intensive services that help increase the value of output and operational efficiency at different stages of the production process. The development of the producer service industry is not only reflected in the range (categories of services) and depth (quality and efficiency of services) of specialised division of labor, but also in the level of division of labor with other industries (Cheng, 2006).[74] Although the development of agriculture, industry and services requires the support of producer services, the producer service industry mainly helps industry at the stage of industrialisation.

Under the assumption that specialisation led to returns to scale and monopolistic market, Francois (1990) deduced the relationship of interactive development between the manufacturing industry and the producer service industry.[31] Developing producer services that function as the high-level input is an important source of improvement in industrial efficiency of output, which can reduce costs of input and improve the quality. It is also conducive to the professionalisation and specialised division of production (Liu, 2006).[34] According to the value chain, the producer service industry is integrated in the industrial value chain in both relational and structural ways, which increases the level of specialisation and achieved potential economies of scale. This would also help achieve higher efficiency of resource allocation and form the coordinated development of the producer service industry and industries to achieve industrial upgrading. In order to improve industrial efficiency, the producer service industry is not only related to the level of specialisation, but also social division of labor, technological level, human resources, social environment and other factors, requiring comprehensive policies to promote the development (Liu et al., 2010).[23] With regards to specialised division of labor, the producer service industry has knowledge spillovers on industry by motivating industrial companies to match their resources, capabilities and technology for the integration in the value chain, so as to promote outsourcing business of services. In this way, the resources and capabilities of industrial enterprises are concentrated in activities with great competitive wess so that the profitability of enterprises can be improved. The spillover effect of the producer service industry on industry is negatively correlated with the geographical distance between enterprises, and it is positively influenced by the perfection of policies (Gu, 2010).[21] As an intermediate input, the producer service industry puts advanced factors, such as intellectual capital, technology and human resources, into the production process to promote the division of the value chain, deepen the specialised division of labor, and increase labor productivity and the added value of products.

Under the modern division of labor, the relationship between the producer service industry and the industry is becoming closer, and they also enhance each other (Lv et al., 2006).[52] Empirical research on Chinese studies showed that production efficiency could be greatly improved if industrial enterprises outsourced less efficient services. More especially, producer services (including software, information services, etc.) with high level of knowledge could have significant impacts on productivity(Yao,2010).[75] The development of the producer service industry could improve its own efficiency,reduce the production cost of industrial products effectively, and promote the overall production efficiency to enhance the competitiveness of industrial enterprises ultimately (Feng, 2009).[18] Although the development of producer services is conducive to the improvement of industrial competitiveness, this role is still relatively weak in China's economic transformation. This is related to the low level of industrial development in China and the lack of motivation for demand in the producer service industry(Gu et al.,2006).[76]

The existing frameworks about mechanisms and impacts of the producer service industry and industry are often discussed on one angle. However,the producer service industry agglomerate in cities,and there are significant differences in mechanisms of the producer service industry at different levels of industrial development, which requires further research to analyse impacts of the producer service industry on industrial transformation and upgrading comprehensively. This book explores impacts of the producer service industry on industrial labor productivity and profitability and the importance of urban institutional environment and market conditions for the development of the producer service industry from the urban level.

Chapter 4.2 Qualitative Research and Basic Hypothesis

Industrial transformation and upgrading is essentially driven by innovation to make production more energy-saving and efficient, including the enhancement of productivity and profitability. The producer service industry improves the industrial production efficiency through the division of labor to outsource services, so as to obtain specialised economy and economies of scale, reduce costs of production and increase the quantity and quality of output. The producer service industry enhances the industrial profitability by integrating itself into the industrial value chain and expanding the original industrial chain for significant transformation from the low end to the high end in the value chain. The producer service industry promotes the industrial transformation and upgrading mainly through these two mutually compatible paths.

Chapter 4.2.1 The Analysis of Labor Productivity

The source of long-term economic growth is the increase in labor productivity, and the greatest improvement in labor productivity is the result of the division of labor (Smith, 1776).[77] The division of labor can strengthen returns to scale through specialisation, and the division of labor depends on the expansion of the market. If the division of labor between production and industries is combined, industries can be regarded as a whole which is internally interconnected through the division of labor. The modern specialised division of labor can mainly improve returns to scale and economies of scope by roundabout production process. The expansion of the market promotes the increasingly specialised division of labor, which would lead to the further expansion of the market. They share mutual causality to promote the division of labor to transform in a cyclic manner for the growth of the modern economy (Young, 1928).[78] According to the framework about division of labor in classical economics, the "externalisation" of the producer service industry is the inevitable result of the deepening of the specialised division of labor and the improvement of marketisation.

With the development of economic globalisation, the market scale has been continuously expanded, the specialised division of labor has gradually deepened, and the production process has become more and more roundabout. The producer service industry puts advanced factors, such as human resources and intellectual capital into the production process, increasing the level of specialisation and diversification in the intermediate investment to make the production process more roundabout. Through the specialisation of production and the deepening investment of capital, it would be more effective to introduce equipment and motivate employees by rewards, which would increase the productivity of labor and other factors, reduce costs of production, and improve production efficiency and industrial competitiveness directly. Under the specialisation of labor, the improvement of labor productivity depends not only on the production efficiency of the production activities but also on the linkages that are established between different production activities and parts. The producer service industry is the "coordinator" between different industries and production activities as an effective way to obtain returns to scale. Human resources and intellectual capital can be gathered, and increasingly specialised and roundabout production process can promote the continuous development of the economy.

The long-term extensive economic growth pattern led to the rapid growth of capacity in China's industrial production and the overall surplus of tangible products, and the profit rate of products continued to decline. In response to changes in the global economic growth and structure of consumers' demand, industrial enterprises have begun to use the producer service industry to find new sources of profits and development. The increasing competition in the market has also led to a significant increase in the demand for producer services by industrial enterprises, which promoted the specialised division of labor in emerging areas in the producer service industry and the continuous separation of the current producer service companies from industrial enterprises. It was reflected as the expansion of the scale and the variety in the producer service industry, and economies of scale and the specialised economy have been enhanced continuously. While reducing costs of intermediate input of services, it would also reduce the production cost of the manufacturing process and support the industrial transformation and upgrading.

Accordingly, the first hypothesis presented in this book is shown below. With the expansion of market capacity and the increase in labor input in the producer service industry, economies of scale and the specialised economy are enhanced constantly, industrial labor productivity would become more efficient with the introduction of advanced equipment and labor motivation with higher rewards.

Chapter 4.2.2 The Analysis of Profitability

In the entire value chain of enterprises, profits at different stages are not the same. The main source of profits actually comes from certain activities in the value chain, and these high-value parts are the strategic activities in the corporate value chain (Porter, 1998).[22] For a company, city or country, the key to gaining competitive advantages in the international market is to use these comparative advantages to capture these strategic activities in the global integration of the value chain (Gu, 2010).[21] In order to enhance competitiveness, enterprises divide the value chain of products, choose to retain strategic activities and outsource some services or production activities to enterprises with comparative advantages to reduce costs and enhance their core competitiveness. By outsourcing or subcontracting producer services, enterprises can also reduce uncertainties and risks so that they can allocate resources on the most competitively strategic part to enhance the flexibility, the ability to control the value chain and expand profit margins. The mutual promotion of the producer services industry and industry in the value chain would promote the continuous optimisation and upgrading of industrial structure(Liu et al.,2010).[23]

Knowledge-intensive producer services lead to product differentiation, as technological innovation often requires a large amount of investment at the early stage. Companies once make innovations, marginal costs are relatively small. Through technological innovation, enterprises differentiate their products and have strong competitiveness, which makes the producer service industry a monopolistic market. The integration of the producer service industry and the modern industries has replaced the traditional industrial growth pattern with stronger control in the value chain and higher profits. In the semiconductor industry, Intel and Flextronics ranked first and second had employees of 83900 and 160000 respectively in 2010. Intel and Flextronics earned US $ 35.1 billion and US $ 24.1 billion as operating income respectively. However, Intel's total profit reached US $ 4.369 billion, which was 230 times that of Flextronics. The main reason was that Intel relied on its technological advantages to control the strategic activities of the value chain in the semiconductor industry with its superior capabilities of making research and development to achieve high profits. Despite the large scale of Flextronics, the profit margins were very limited in manufacturing and the ability to respond to external changes was relatively weak. Among the 100 largest multinational companies, service companies increased from 12 in 1995 to 53 in 2010. 15 companies had profit margins greater than 10%, and nine of them were producer service companies, including 4 banks, 4 companies of telecommunication and one company of information technology services.

Since the reform and opening up, China has absorbed a large amount of foreign direct investment and accepted the industrial transfer of developed countries by increasing the degree of dependence on foreign trade. It promoted the rapid growth of traditional industries that were labor intensive, low added value and high consumption of resources. However, this development pattern at the low end of the value chain has been increasingly subject to pressure from slower pace of global economic growth, deteriorating ecological system, and rising costs of factors. Industrial exports have faced severe challenges and lacked the capacity for sustainable development in the low-end and homogenised competition. In the international financial crisis in 2008, China's export-oriented industrial enterprises suffered major impacts, declining competitiveness, poorer profits and even bankruptcy. At present, China's industries are in the process of transformation and upgrading. The development of the producer service industry can help solve the shortcomings of industrial enterprises in lacking technological innovations, designing products, researching and developing advantages, and managing companies. The development of the producer service industry can also promote the rise of industrial enterprises to the high end of the value chain, which is the key to China's industrial transformation and upgrading.

Accordingly, the second hypothesis presented in this book is shown below. Industrial enterprises separate the less efficient producer services through outsourcing services, and focus on the strategic activities with competitive advantages to enhance the ability to integrate the value chain and profit margins of industries.

Chapter 4.2.3 The Analysis of Market Scale and Policies

With the deepening social division of labor and the improvement of specialisation, the types and scale of the producer service industry continue to expand. While reducing production costs, it would also cause an increase in various transaction costs, which offsets some benefits of the higher efficiency by the division of labor. Since most producer services companies are contract-intensive, production and transactions would involve more intensive and complex contractual arrangements. When other conditions are the same, the better the maintenance system over contracts in a city, the less opportunistic behaviour of both sides in transactions, and the quicker development of the producer service industry (Wang et al., 2007). [20] Without the complete institutional environment, the provision of producer services within companies may be the best choice for the lowest risk. The reduction of outsourcing services would fundamentally restrict the growth of the demand for producer services, and it would be difficult to benefit from the agglomeration of the urban economy. Cities need to build a complete market system so that professional producer service enterprises can reduce transaction costs through specialised division of labor, economies of scale, economies of scope and institutional innovation. If a city's producer service industry is not competitive enough, it would affect the competitiveness of local industrial enterprises, and thus hinder the overall economic development of the city. Therefore, combining the Coase Theorem with Smith-Yong Theorem, Adam Smith's concepts of "limiting division of labor by the market" can be concluded to "limiting division of labor by the direction and pace of institutional changes".[78]

In international cities, such as New York, London and Tokyo, there are strict protective means for contracts, transparent administrative environment, orderly competition in industries and trust between institutions. With the rapid development of information technology, industrial enterprises outsourced producer services or transformed them to become service enterprises, and organisational changes continued to reduce costs and improve industrial competitiveness. At present, IBM, GE and other companies have transformed from computing and automobile manufacturing enterprises to enterprises that provide information technology services and diversified financial business. The development of "providing services of manufacturing" or "service-oriented manufacturing" achieved a high degree of integration between products and services. Enterprises provide producer services to each other for integration of resources in the value chain. Enterprises develop in an efficient and innovative manner by forming industrial clusters in developed cities (Feng, 2009).[18]

China's industries still stay in the low-end competition in manufacturing. In addition, the overall market environment of the cities has not been standardised, and the motivation for industrial enterprises to outsource services is not strong. These are the main reasons that restrict the producer service industry and affect the industrial transformation and upgrading. Large cities have stronger economic capacity of influencing the surrounding area and higher economic density, and they can have the multiplier effect on the development of the producer service industry through regional cooperation. Large cities can also provide transportation facilities, developed information networks and other necessary conditions for the development of the producer service industry. In the context of economic globalisation and regional integration, large cities have attracted more elements to agglomerate to participate more in international and regional industrial division of labor. It should be pointed out that state-owned capital has obtained great control in the fields of producer services, such as telecommunications and banking, to form a certain degree of monopoly. This is not conducive to the process of marketisation in cities, and it would weaken the interactive development between the producer service industry and industry. This is especially obvious in cities with smaller size of market and lower degree of openness.

Accordingly, the third hypothesis presented in this book is shown below. The perfect market-oriented environment and a large scale of market economy play a key role in increasing the effective demand for the producer service industry, and the role of the producer service industry in industrial transformation and upgrading in developed large cities is more obvious.

Chapter 4.3 Data Models and Empirical Analysis

The theoretical analysis above deduces mechanisms of the producer service industry on industrial labor productivity and profit rate, as well as the preconditions for these mechanisms. Three hypotheses are also proposed accordingly.The following part would use the econometric model for empirical research based on the analysis above.

Chapter 4.3.1 Data Models, Variable Determination and Findings

In the process of industrial transformation and upgrading, the producer service industry puts intellectual capital, human resources and technology into the production process to increase the quantity and quality of output and integrate them into the value chain and manufacturing processes, promote the application of new technologies, the development of new products, and continuously increase the added value of products.Therefore, impacts of the producer service industry on industrial transformation and upgrading would be reflected as the increase in labor productivity and profit margins caused by the specialised division of labor and higher position in the value chain.This book compares the two variables of industrial labor productivity and profit rate as dependent variables. Due to the complexity of economic activities, in addition to identifying the producer service industry as an important explanatory variable, it also introduces control variables, such as industrial fixed assets per capita, the proportion of foreign direct investment in the gross domestic product, the proportion of scientific education in fiscal expenditure, and the average wage level of employees, to conduct a more comprehensive analysis of how the producer service industry would influence industrial transformation and upgrading. Of course, the conditions for the development of the producer service industry, such as economic density, the degree of dependence on foreign trade and free market, are also the key issues to be considered in the construction of the econometric model.

Most of the producer services industry and industry agglomerate in cities. Therefore, using data of cities is better than that of provinces to reflect the mechanism and impacts of the producer service industry on industry under different economic development levels. The data used in this book are from 284 municipal districts in China from 2003 to 2010 (due to the limitation of the organisational system, the figures in Longnan, Gansu and Zhongwei, Ningxia Hui Autonomous Region are not included and analysed). This book classifies cities according to the population of more than 5 million, from 2 million to 5 million, from 1 million to 2 million, from 500000 to 1 million, and less than 500000 into central cities, megacities, large cities, medium-sized cities, and small and medium-sized cities. Beijing, Tianjin, Shanghai, Nanjing, Guangzhou, Wuhan, Chongqing, Chengdu, Xi' an and Shenyang are central cities with the population of more than 5 million. According to the classification of the producer service industry in the "12th Five-Year Plan", this book selects five areas in the producer service industry, such as finance, transportation, warehousing and postal services, information transmission, computing services and software, scientific research, technical services and geological exploration, leasing and business services. The fixed-effect model is used to demonstrate preconditions and impacts of the producer service industry on industrial labor productivity and profit rate.

This book uses a logarithmic model to measure the percentage change in the explanatory variable and the result in the dependent variable. The specific econometric model is as follows:

Model I: $$\ln ILP_{it} = \alpha_0 + \alpha_1 \ln PS_{it} + \alpha_2 \ln FA_{it} + \alpha_3 \ln FDI_{it} + \alpha_4 \ln SE_{i(t-1)} + \alpha_5 \ln W_{it} + \varepsilon_{it} \tag{4.1}$$

Model II: $$\ln IPR_{it} = \beta_0 + \beta_1 \ln PS_{it} + \beta_2 \ln FA_{it} + \beta_3 \ln FDI_{it} + \beta_4 \ln SE_{i(t-1)} + \varepsilon_{it} \tag{4.2}$$

Model III: $$\ln PS_{it} = \delta_0 + \delta_1 \ln GDP_{it} + \delta_2 \ln FDI_{it} + \delta_3 \ln GOV_{it} + \varepsilon_{it} \tag{4.3}$$

i represents cities, and t represents time. ILP is the labor productivity of industry, and its increase reflects the improvement of returns to scale under the specialisation of labor. IPR is the profit margin of industry, and its increase reflects the rise of industrial enterprises in the value chain. PS is the proportion of employment in the producer service industry compared to the total employment, reflecting the degree of specialised division of labor in the producer service industry. The higher the proportion, the better the specialised division of labor in the producer service industry. FA is the industrial fixed assets per capita, reflecting the composition of capital. FDI is the proportion of foreign direct investment in the gross domestic product, reflecting impacts of foreign direct investment on the competition of the industrial market. SE is the proportion of science and education in urban financial expenditure, reflecting the development level of scientific technology and education. It means the improvement of workers' quality of and skills, which plays an important role in promoting industrial transformation and upgrading. After considering long-term impacts of investing science education on the economy, this book uses indicators that lag behind the first phase. W is the wage level per capita, reflecting the incentives of rewards for workers in the industrial production process. GDP is the economic density in the area of cities, reflecting impacts of economic agglomeration and expansion of market scale on the development of the producer service industry. GOV is the proportion of local fiscal revenue in the gross domestic product, reflecting the degree of governmental impacts on the economy. The lower the proportion, the higher the degree of freedom in the market.

Chapter 4.3.2 Empirical Analysis of Results

The results of empirical analysis are mainly carried out from three aspects: labor productivity, industrial profit rate and conditions for the development of the producer service industry.

(1) The first is the analysis of labor productivity. The producer

service industry has a significant positive correlation with the increase of industrial labor productivity in central cities and megacities. In the calculation of Model I, the coefficient of labor input in the producer service industry is 0.313 and 0.149 in central cities and megacities, which means that the labor productivity of the manufacturing industry would increase by 0.313% and 0.149% for every 1% increase in the labor input of the producer service industry (see Table 4.1). The industries of central cities, such as Beijing and Shanghai, and megacities, such as Shenzhen and Hangzhou, have begun the high-end development, so the demand for the producer service industry is fairly large. The agglomeration of the producer service industry in central cities and megacities is conducive to the formation of a market for specialised producer services to fully meet the needs of industrial transformation and upgrading. The producer service industry greatly promotes the intensification of production by improving the quality of intermediate inputs, which is conducive to the transformation of traditional industries and the development of strategic emerging industries, making output more efficient. In other types of cities, the producer service industry has negative impacts on manufacturing efficiency to a small extent, as China's financial insurance, railway and air transport, telecommunications, postal services and other areas in the producer service industry benefit greatly from the market monopoly by administrative means. The problem of high prices and low quality is particularly prominent in small cities. It limits the development of private companies in the producer service industry, and increases the operating costs of industrial enterprises inevitably.

Table 4.1 Empirical analysis of factors affecting industrial labor productivity in different cities

Explanatory variable	Central cities	Megacities	Large cities	Medium-sized cities	Small and medium-sized cities
cons	-0.352*** (-4.73)	-5.169*** (-9.52)	-4.398*** (-12.73)	-5.277*** (-12.98)	-6.480*** (-5.74)
PS	0.313*** (1.47)	0.149*** (1.55)	-0.022** (-1.33)	-0.067** (-1.22)	-0.018** (-1.12)
FA	0.202** (1.67)	0.293*** (5.08)	0.369*** (12.82)	0.236*** (9.19)	0.341*** (6.94)
FDI	0.090** (1.81)	0.014** (1.61)	-0.035** (-2.39)	0.021** (2.04)	0.003* (1.13)
$SE_{(-1)}$	0.127** (1.50)	0.095*** (2.08)	0.014* (1.35)	0.067** (2.35)	0.083** (1.07)
W	0.574*** (4.51)	0.881*** 14.79	0.730*** 19.44	0.813*** (15.21)	0.874*** (5.64)
R^2_{adj}	0.9500	0.9352	0.8757	0.9130	0.8461
F value	103.75	256.73	310.17	447.50	103.79
Number of cities	10	30	78	110	56
Number of samples	80	240	624	880	448

Note: t in parentheses represents "test value". *** indicates significant results at 1% level, ** indicates significant results at 5% level, and * indicates significant results at 10% level. The calculation was completed with the use of measurement software, stata 12.

The popularisation of production technology, the use of advanced equipment, and the improvement of workers' quality stabilised the contribution of industrial fixed assets per capita to labor productivity. The increase of investment in fixed assets world be an important factor for the improvement of industrial production efficiency. Foreign direct investment has positive spillover effects in central cities and megacities, which is caused by the participation of foreign investors to improve the market structure and stimulate the vitality of the market in central cities, so as to form industrial clusters in central cities and megacities for specialisation and economies of scale. Foreign direct investment is attracted to the manufacturing industry of large cities, and industrial enterprises with weak competitiveness face with the pressure of survival and fierce competition, which even increases the bankruptcy of enterprises and unemployment rate. In medium-sized cities, the introduction of foreign direct investment can play a leading role in local industries, promoting local industrial enterprises to provide supporting facilities and improve production efficiency. In the small and medium-sized cities, impacts of foreign direct investment are relatively small, due to the low degree of economic openness. Proportion of science education in fiscal expenditure has positive impacts on industrial labor productivity. It should be pointed out that the driving force of spending fiscal expenditure on science and education is gradually reduced in less developed cities. The main reason is that central cities and mega-cities have good market environment and opportunities, which are obvious advantagesous to attract high-end talents and adapt technologies for the market. Rewarding employees gives a very obvious incentive to promote the production process, and it is also the most important factor for the improvement of labor productivity. However, this effect is relatively weak in central cities, because the wage level is relatively high in central cities and the incentive for wages is not as apparent as other cities.

(2) The second is the analysis of the industrial profit rate. Compared with labor productivity, the producer service industry has positive impacts on the industrial profit rate, but the impacts are relatively small. The results of Model II show that the producer service industry mainly helps auxiliary activities of industrial enterprises. Profit margins are increased through outsourcing services to reduce production costs, which is more apparent in smaller cities (see Table 4.2). In smaller cities, industrial enterprises are constrained by the system, producer services are often provided internally. This cannot increase corporate profits, but become a burden for the development of enterprises. Only through outsourcing services can companies focus on production processes so that efficiency and profitability can be improved. In central cities, megacities and large cities, the producer service industry has fewer impacts on the improvement of the industrial profit margin. China's industry basically relies on hiring cheap labor and expanding the scale of production to obtain low profits in manufacturing, and the low-end manufacturing industry clearly has a shortage of demand for emerging producer services. The international financial crisis caused tremendous impacts on China's industrial exports and resulted in a difficult situation. The low-level industrial development pattern was not conducive to the effective integration of

the value chain and the introduction of advanced production factors into the production process, resulting to insufficient conditions for the development of the producer service industry. This was the most important reason that limited the level of industrial development in the producer service industry.

Table 4.2 Empirical analysis of factors affecting industrial profit rate in different cities

Explanatory variable	Central cities	Megacities	Large cities	Medium-sized cities	Small and medium-sized cities
cons	0.891** (1.60)	0.250*** (1.27)	0.836*** (1.53)	−0.639** (1.23)	−1.651** (1.52)
PS	0.014*** (2.03)	0.052** (1.16)	0.092** (1.46)	0.215*** (2.12)	0.612*** (2.60)
FA	−0.105** (−1.33)	0.406*** (3.28)	0.300*** (4.36)	0.238*** (2.76)	0.080** (1.64)
FDI	0.057** (1.42)	−0.122** (−1.63)	−0.012* (−1.28)	0.004** (1.11)	−0.067* (1.25)
SE(−1)	0.161*** (1.98)	0.066** (1.44)	0.123** (1.01)	0.147*** (2.29)	0.206*** (1.91)
R^2_{adj}	0.9066	0.8768	0.8791	0.9166	0.9495
F value	100.84	95.96	95.07	410.54	103.39
Number of cities	10	30	78	110	56
Number of samples	80	240	624	880	448

Note: t in parentheses represents "test value". *** indicates significant results at 1% level, ** indicates significant results at 5% level, and * indicates significant results at 10% level. The calculation was completed with the use of measurement software, stata 12.

Although industrial fixed assets per capita have relatively great impacts on the promotion of labor productivity, the increase in the quantity of output does not stimulate the increase in industrial profit margins significantly. Therefore, relying on the expansion of scale cannot fundamentally realise the transformation of China from a large industrial country to a competitive industrial country. This can also be reflected by the changes in industrial output per capita and industrial profit rate (see Figure 4.1). From 2003 to 2010, China's industrial output value per capita increased sharply year by year, while the industrial profit rate showed fluctuations in a W-shaped curve. In the financial crisis in 2008, the industrial profit margins fell sharply, due to the changes in the external environment. Of course, the figures of industrial output value per capita and industrial profit margins are relatively high in cities with higher levels of development. Since foreign direct investment only changes the fierce competition in the market, it cannot change the position of China's industrial enterprises as manufacturers in the industrial chain, so the impacts on the industrial profit rate are limited. Producer services of foreign-invested industrial enterprises are mainly provided by the headquarters of multinational corporations, which would not generate substantial demand for local producer services in the market. Due to the insufficient support of the local producer service industry to local industries, the competitiveness of domestic industries is lower than that of foreign-invested industries inevitably. As a result, China's industry has been at the low end of the global value chain for a long time and become dependent upon the low-end industrial development pattern. The investment in science and education can promote enterprises to make innovations and improve workers' quality. This measure has long-term and positive impacts on the integration and development of industrial and the producer service industry and the improvement of industrial competitiveness.

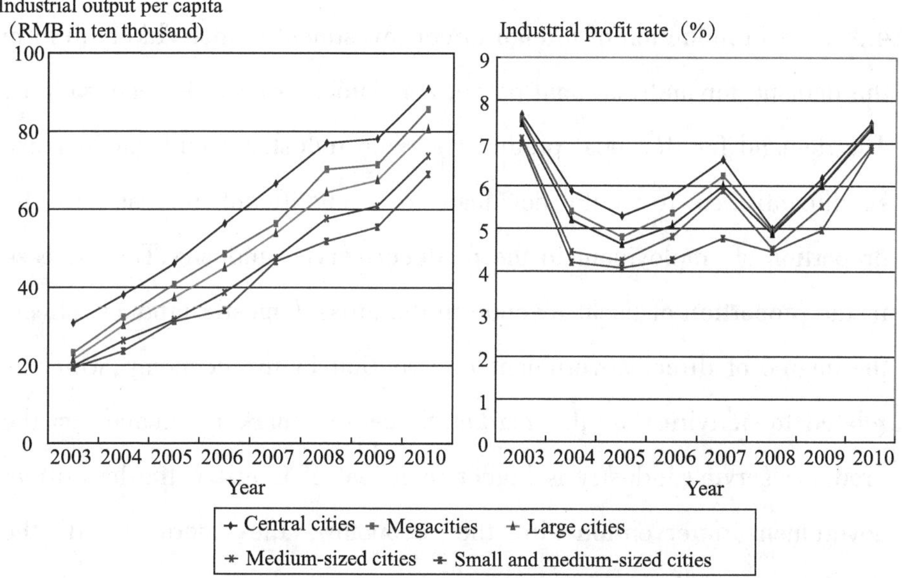

Figure 4.1 Changes in industrial output per capita and industrial profit margins in different cities from 2003 to 2010

(3) The third is the analysis of the conditions to develop the producer service industry. The development of the producer service industry is highly correlated with the population density and economic density of cities. Large cities that gather a large amount of labor, capital, resources, technology and industries are the basic spatial carriers for the development of the producer service industry.The results

of Model III show that the development of the producer service industry is closely related to the economic density of cities, because the producer service industry is a typical demand-driven industry. Only the expansion of the market scale can promote the increasingly specialised division of labor and the division of the value chain, creating the necessary preconditions for outsourcing business of producer services (see Table 4.3). The introduction of foreign direct investment is more likely to form the demand for multinational parent companies or service organisations. The demand for the local producer service industry would not increase significantly, so it would not lead to a significant increase in the proportion of employment in the producer service industry. The increase in the proportion of fiscal revenue in the gross domestic product reflects the degree of direct government intervention in the economy, which is related to activities in the market. Since the market demand for the producer service industry is higher than that of industry, the less direct government intervention in the economy, the more rapid the development of the producer service industry.

Table 4.3 Empirical analysis of the conditions for the development of the producer service industry in different cities

Explanatory variable	Central cities	Megacities	Large cities	Medium-sized cities	Small and medium-sized cities
cons	2.218*** (1.60)	2.590*** (6.25)	2.26*** (8.58)	1.609*** (1.23)	1.830*** (1.52)
GDP	0.122*** (2.03)	0.116*** (1.81)	0.123*** (1.49)	0.125*** (2.12)	0.134*** (2.60)

续表

Explanatory variable	Central cities	Megacities	Large cities	Medium-sized cities	Small and medium-sized cities
FDI	-0.047 ** (-1.33)	-0.27 ** (-1.77)	-0.003 * (-1.35)	0.011 *** (2.76)	0.006 ** (1.64)
GOV	-0.108 *** (1.98)	0.046 ** (1.87)	0.022 ** (1.80)	0.068 *** (2.29)	0.037 *** (1.91)
R^2_{adj}	0.9580	0.9281	0.8337	0.8812	0.9504
F value	23.81	22.26	11.31	16.39	13.49
Number of cities	10	30	78	110	56
Number of samples	80	240	624	880	448

Note: t in parentheses represents "test value". *** indicates significant results at 1% level, ** indicates significant results at 5% level, and * indicates significant results at 10% level. The calculation was completed with the use of measurement software, stata 12.

Chapter 4.4 The Summary

The research in this chapter shows that the producer service industry can give full play to economies of scale and promote the specialised division of labor in the relatively developed and large cities, and improve the labor productivity of industry. However, under the monopolistic competition, the producer service industry would increase the operating cost of enterprises, and has no positive effect on the improvement of industrial labor productivity. The current impacts of the producer service industry on the industrial profit rate are mainly reflected in the reduction of production costs by providing auxiliary services to increase profit margins, but improving the position of industrial enterprises in the value chain still needs better conditions. The producer service industry is demand-driven. The expansion of the economic scale and the improvement of market systems in central cities and megacities would help promote the integration of the producer service industry and the industry, so producer service companies agglomerate in metropolises for the development.

In the process of economic globalisation, China's transformation from a "large industrial country" to a "competitive industrial country" must rely on the development of the producer service industry to further promote industrial transformation and upgrading. However, the development of China's producer service industry is relatively lagging behind and cannot meet the needs of industrial development. Therefore, it is necessary to promote the development of the producer service industry as the strategic focus of optimising and upgrading the industrial structure, and take practical and effective measures to formulate policies for institutional environment which is conducive to the development of the producer service industry.

Firstly, we need to accelerate the institutional reform of the producer service industry. With the development of economic globalisation, the producer service industry would be open to foreign investment gradually. Foreign direct investment would intensify market competition and pose threats to the development of China's producer service industry. At present, it is necessary to speed up the institutional reform of state-owned enterprises in the producer service industry, improve business management and innovate patterns to provide services for the competitiveness of enterprises. At the same time, we must reduce unnecessary industrial controls, reduce barriers to market entry, and encourage and guide private companies into the producer service industry. We need to give the equal treatment and position to private companies in the market, strengthen the mechanism in competition, and gradually break the unreasonable monopoly in industries for industrial transformation and upgrading sustainable economic development.

Secondly, we need to standardise the market system of the producer service industry. The producer service industry is contract-intensive, and it is necessary to establish a standardised market system to maintain capacities of making innovations in the producer service industry, including complete industrial standards and regulation of market behaviour in producer service companies. We must rationally guide the development of new producer services and establish a unified, open, competitive and orderly market for producer services. The urban market system would effectively reduce the uncertainty caused by the division of labor or the value chain, and reduce the risk of cooperation in outsourcing services and transaction costs in the market, attracting to implement strategies of outsourcing services.

In addition, we must develop policies to support for the producer service industry. China's industrial policies mainly support industry but not the producer service industry. Compared to industrial companies, there are high operating costs for producer service companies, such as prices of water, gas, land, the difficulty of financing and tax burden. Therefore, it is necessary to promote the pilot reform of the national producer service industry with lower tax and fewer requirements for loan to reduce financing costs, and enjoy equal benefits in the use of resources. We need to especially encourage large-scale and high-quality producer service enterprises with higher reputation to implement mergers and acquisitions across regions and industries according to market mechanisms. We should also encourage them to become bigger and more competitive to improve the competitiveness of China's producer service enterprises.

Finally, we need to coordinate the development of the producer service industry. The underdevelopment of urbanisation and the separation of industrial layout in China have weakened the demand for the producer service industry, resulting in the lack of necessary conditions to develop the producer service industry and support the industrial chain effectively. Producer services that could have been provided through outsourcing have to be completed within industrial enterprises, because of the lower degree of specialisation or the higher price. Therefore, it is necessary to promote the formation of industrial structure based on producer services in central cities and the megacities. Developing clusters of producer service companies can promote the separation of the producer service industry and the industry, and encourage industrial enterprises to move to the surrounding area of large cities or other cities. This can create conditions for the relocation and agglomeration of the producer service industry and industrial enterprises to achieve structural optimisation and upgrading in industrial transfer. Large cities can influence the surrounding area through the producer service industry, while small and medium-sized cities use the vertical division of industries and the derivation of the industrial chain to benefit from large-scale industries, so as to form the development pattern of integration, division of labor, and complementary advantages among cities.

Chapter Five

Impacts of Developing the Producer Service Industry on the Optimisation of Urban Employment Structure

Since the reform and opening up, relying on the low - cost of production factors, such as labor, land and capital, and the huge market potential released by economic growth, China has rapidly expanded the capacities of manufacturing goods by encouraging exports and attracting foreign direct investment. Manufacturing has become the most important industrial sector providing employment and absorbed a large amount of unskilled labor. However, due to the rise in the exchange rate of Chinese currency, increasing costs of labor and land, and the external changes of the international financial crisis in 2008 and the European sovereign debt crisis, the growth of China's manufacturing industry has begun to slow down, the pressure on the job market has increased sharply, and structural contradictions have become increasingly prominent. In the case of slower economic growth, employment is the biggest issue of people's living conditions and a key indicator to measure the quality of China's economic operations. In 2014, China's economy grew by 7.4%, and there were 13.22 million new jobs in urban areas. The unemployment rate maintained at 5.1%, and consumer prices rose by 2%. These four indicators can be combined to show that the Chinese economy continued to develop in a reasonable manner. The economic growth rate declined in 2014. According to Okun's law, the slowdown in economic growth means that the ability to absorb employment would be weakened. However, when the proportion of the secondary industry in the gross domestic product decreases, China's employment rate is generally stable, and the capability of creating new jobs is better than expectations in urban areas. This is mainly caused by the rapid development of the service industry. The service industry has become the main channel for absorbing employment. In 2011, the proportion of employment in the tertiary industry in China surpassed the primary industry for the first time and ranked first, which has increased year by year since then. Compared with other sectors, service industries are characterised by large employment elasticity, high intensity of labor, technology and knowledge. It has unique advantages in absorbing labor with different qualities, and Alibaba has created nearly 10 million jobs and recruited employees from different background.

Chapter 5. 1 Developing the Producer Service Industry to Solve the Shortage of Labor

Since 2004, China's coastal cities have experienced labor shortages before and after the Spring Festival. In recent years, the "labor shortage" has also occurred in the central and western regions. After the Spring Festival in 2012, the ratio of demand in Guangdong Province (market demand for labor/number of job seekers) was between 1.15 and 1.18, and the shortage would be more than 3 million people if the number of 20 million employees was taken as the base for calculation.[79] Although the specific figures of China's labor shortages need further calculation, the era of low-cost labor would gradually end with the arrival of the "Lewis turning point". At the same time, many college students have to graduate from school and become unemployed. Since the expansion of enrolment in 1999, Chinese universities have changed from elite education to mass education. In 2011, the number of college graduates reached 6.6 million. The national employment rate of university graduates in 2008, 2009 and 2010 reached 85.5%, 86.6% and 89. 6% respectively. Although the employment rate of college students has improved in recent years, the total number of unemployed graduates in three years was 2.28 million.[80]

As cities are the area for the concentration and development of non-agricultural industries, the labor force would be mainly absorbed by urban sectors in China's rapid economic growth (Cai, 2010).[81] The serious imbalance in the job market is evident in cities, especially in large cities. This not only restricts the sustainable development of the urban economy, but also makes the unemployment rate and income gap of cities at a high level. It would also become the main reason for a series of social problems that cause uneven distribution of urban public resources and increase in the crime rate, so employment should be the priority in the urban economic and social development. Developing the producer service industry can realise reasonable specialised division of labor in the urban system, reconstruct the spatial layout for industries and promote the upgrading of the industrial structure in the transfer. This would be an effective way to alleviate the structural contradictions in the job market, guiding labor from the different background to flow orderly to various industries and cities.

In classical economics, the optimisation of employment structure and the transformation of industrial structure are closely related. William Petty (1690) found that the relative income difference between industries was the main reason for the transfer of labor between industries. More especially, agriculture provided lower incomes than manufacturing, and manufacturing provided lower incomes than business, so the labor force tended to move from agriculture to manufacturing and to business. Clark (1941) further pointed out that economic development and rising income levels led to the transfer of labor from agriculture to industry, and to service industries. The proportion of agriculture declined gradually, and the proportion of employment and output in industry and service industries increased. What's more, the propotion of employment in service industries increased with the highest speed. This is called the "Petty Clark theory".[82] With the increase in income per capita, the proportion of employment in service industries would continue to rise, which is the general trend in the economic development of countries around the world (Chenery, 1986).[83] In the modern economic growth, the economic structure dominated by the manufacturing industry would shift to the economic structure dominated by service industries gradually. Furthermore, the structure of service industries would change from traditional service industries to modern service industries led by the producer service industry. The commercial and financial industries would become the largest sector in service industries (Kuznets, 1966).[84] China's relevant empirical research also confirmed that service industries would be the main channel for absorbing the labor force (Li, 2003 [85]; Zhang, 2006 [86]).

In the process of economic reorganisation, China's job market also experienced fundamental changes. In 2013, the total gross domestic product reached RMB 56.88 trillion and ranked second in the world. The gross domestic product per capita reached RMB 41804.71, which was US $ 6747 according to the cross-country comparable price indices of the International Monetary Fund. Based on the World Bank's standards, China has become an upper-middle-income country, as the gross domestic product per capita has already exceeded US $ 6000. However, the advent of the "Lewis turning point" gradually offset the demographic dividend caused by the dual economic structure at the early stage of reform and opening up, and comparative advantages of low-cost labor disappeared gradually (Cai, 2010).[81] China's low-end manufacturing industry has grown slower and slower under the pressure of competition from "re-industrialisation" in developed countries and the "homogeneity" in emerging economies. It would be difficult to increase the capabilities of absorbing the labor force by increasing wages (Wang & Ma, 2011).[87] The underdevelopment of the advanced manufacturing and producer service industries caused difficulties of forming large demand for specialised workers. In addition, the market monopoly formed by government intervention led to insufficient competition and continued to widen the income gap between industries. The income inequality between industries also contributed to the greater income gap of urban residents in China (Chen et al., 2010).[88]

In order to improve the capacities of absorbing the labor force in the economic growth process, some long-lasting and effective measures are needed, including the reduction of mobility barriers for the labor force to improve the mechanism, the enhancement of training systems to strengthen the education level and professional quality of workers, less government intervention in attracting investment and economic development to promote the development of high-employment industries in the market. These should be important government policies for the economy(Cai et al.,2004 [89]; Chen et al.,2010 [88]; Lu & Ou,2011 [90]). Although China's overall employment elasticity has been declining,the employment elasticity of service industries,especially in the producer service industry, was significantly higher than that of primary and second sectors(Liu & Liu,2008).[91] As the intermediate investment in other industries,the producer service industry has great impacts on employment directly and indirectly. While increasing the employment of the producer service industry,it would create a lot more job opportunities in other industries, thereby increasing the total employment rate(Tian,2010).[92] Therefore,accelerating the development of service industries, increasing the proportion of the producer service industry in the industrial structure, and making the producer service industry the leading industry of the national economy and the main channel for attracting new workers in urban and rural areas are the key to promoting full employment in China.(Wu & Hu,2011).[93]

The existing theories mainly analyse the trend of transforming industrial structure and employment structure, and point out that the producer service industry would be the main industry in China to absorb the labor force in the future.However,the current problem of China's employment is essentially a structural contradiction, and the key issue is where the labor force should be.That is to say,further studies need to be focused on the overall expansion and orderly flow of the labor force through the spatial and structural optimisation in industries.In addition to increasing labor demand by the development,it is more important for the producer service industry to form a rational urban system through the spatial reorganisation of industrial activities, so as to give full play to advantages of specialised division of labor for sustainable economic development in cities.

Chapter 5.2 The Mechanism of the Producer Service Industry to Promote the Optimisation of Urban Employment Structure

The main reasons for the structural contradictions in the employment market in China are as follows. Firstly, due to the dual economic structure, workers from rural areas cannot obtain urban household registration and the corresponding working benefits and social welfare in urban areas, thus reducing the labor supply in cities. In addition, the increase in costs of labor mobility and support payments caused by ageing population also caused more contradictions between supply and demand in the job market. Secondly, due to the information asymmetry in the job market, workers from rural areas and college students may choose jobs blindly in urban areas, leading to the shortage of labor. The disorderly flow of labor has forced many cities to face social problems caused by excessive migrant populations. Thirdly, China's industry has a large proportion of labor-intensive industries. They have been at the low end of the value chain for a long time. The weakening comparative advantages of factors decreased profit margins of enterprises, limiting the increase in wages to motivate workers effectively.

Therefore, solving the employment issues in our country requires to combine the expansion of the total employment market, the orderly flow of the labor force and the continuous improvement of wages, and the producer service industry also plays a key role in it.

Chapter 5.2.1 the Analyses of the Overall Employment

Although the growth rate tends to decline, China still has a large population, and the overall scale and growth of the job market is still large. In 2011, the number of employed people nationwide reached 764.2 million, with 12.21 million new jobs in urban areas. In the promotion of industrialisation, large-scale standardised production methods have been widely adopted, and the use of assembly lines greatly promoted the development of division of labor. Enterprises expanded rapidly, industrial products were quickly integrated into the lives of most families, and the manufacturing industry became the main channel for employment. With the development of the economy, the further specialised division of labor, the production process became more and more roundabout, requiring more specialised and diversified producer services. Therefore, the ability of service industries to provide employment opportunities has gradually increased. Under the economic globalisation and popularisation of information technology, it is possible to reorganise the value chain, and the producer service industry becomes the key to controlling the industrial chain in international cities. Since the producer service industry is a knowledge-intensive industry, it requires a large amount of specialised labor in the development process, so it is also conducive to improving workers' quality and increasing the capacity of absorbing the labor force. At the same time, the producer service industry enhances the connection with different industries and promote the integration for the transformation of traditional industries and the rise of strategic emerging industries through investing intellectual capital, human resources and technology into the production process. The development of these industries would lead to the expansion of the overall employment rate and the improvement of employees' quality.

At the same time, the upgrading of the manufacturing industry would increase the demand for producer services. The improvement of employees' quality would help increase the quantity and quality of producer services. The interaction between industries continues to drive the increase in the total employment rate and the improvement of labor quality. Employment elasticity reflects the capacities of absorbing the labor force in economic growth. Higher employment elasticity means that economic growth can bring more employment opportunities, and more achievements of economic growth can be shared by workers. In the market economy, companies usually maximise profits by selecting technologies based on relative prices of factors to produce goods. Changes in relative prices of factors are inseparable from the level of economic development. The change of employment elasticity usually comes with the transformation of economic development. At the early stage of industrialisation, capital is more scarce and expensive than labor, so companies would prefer to use labor, and the employment elasticity of economic growth is relatively high. As the level of economic development and labor productivity continue to increase, capital becomes less scarce gradually, and prices of labor are gradually increasing. Manufacturing companies at the lower end of the value chain would choose to use more capital and technology, and employment elasticity would gradually decrease. The producer service industry at the high end of the value chain would attract more professionals, and the employment elasticity would rise. The experience of developed countries showed that employment elasticity would increase with rapid economic growth, and industry would become the largest sector to absorb the labor force. As the economy develops, service industries gradually replace industry as the main channel of absorbing the labor force, and the overall employment elasticity would decrease after the economy becomes mature (Piacentini & Pini, 2000).[94]

Employment elasticity is the percentage change in the number of employees for each percentage change in economic growth under the premise that other factors remain unchanged, which is expressed as the ratio of growth rate in employment to growth rate in the economy. The greater the elasticity of employment, the greater number of employees that economic growth can absorb. The formula for employment elasticity is shown below:

$$\varepsilon_t = \frac{(L_{t+1} - L_t)/L_t}{(Y_{t+1} - Y_t)/Y_t} \tag{5.1}$$

However, by dividing the growth rate of employment calculated at two different periods by the economic growth rate, the overall elasticity cannot be calculated for consecutive years, and there are also errors caused by data fluctuations. This is not conducive to the prediction of employment growth in the future.

In order to more accurately estimate the elasticity of employment and make it useful for prediction, this book uses the following nonlinear model between economic growth and employment:

$$L_{it} = AY_{it}^{\alpha}e^{u} \tag{5.2}$$

The natural logarithm are taken from both sides of the formula to get a double logarithmic model:

$$\ln(L_{it}) = \ln A + \alpha\ln(Y_{it}) + u \tag{5.3}$$

L represents the number of employees, A is a constant coefficient, Y is GDP , α is the employment elasticity, and u represents random errors. As the data model can better integrate the information of time series and cross-section data, it has high value of application through taking multiple sections in time series and selecting samples to observe and form the database. Fixed-effect models are often used in data analysis to reduce the effects of individual exceptions, so the book uses the data from 284 municipal districts in China from 2003 to 2010 (collected from the China City Statistical Yearbook between 2004 and 2011). The fixed-effect model is used in stata12 to analyse the employment elasticity in industries and cities with different levels.

The employment elasticity is different in cities with different economic development levels, so this book classifies cities according to the population of more than 5 million, from 2 million to 5 million, from 1 million to 2 million, from 500000 to 1 million, and less than 500000 as central cities, megacities, large cities, medium-sized cities, and small and medium-sized cities. According to the classification of the producer service industry in the "12th Five-Year Plan", this book selects five areas in the producer service industry, such as finance, transportation, warehousing and postal services, information transmission, computing services and software, scientific research, technical services and geological exploration, leasing and business services.

Overall, central cities and megacities have higher employment elasticity. As cities become smaller, employment elasticity gradually decreases. The employment elasticity of central cities and megacities reached 0.175 and 0.212 respectively, that is, for every percentage increase in the gross domestic product, the total employment rate would increase by 0.175% and 0.212%. Central cities, such as Beijing and Shanghai, and megacities, such as Shenzhen and Hangzhou, have a high level of economic development as the centre of the urban system or the regional economy to provide higher wages for the labor force and guide talents to megacities. Moreover, central cities and megacities can achieve economies of scale through sharing, matching, and learning. Continuous self-reinforcement and industrial agglomeration can attract talents to gather together (Gill & Kharas, 2007).[95]

Table 5.1 Estimation results of employment elasticity in different industries and cities from 2003 to 2010

	Cities	Employment elasticity	R^2	R^2_{adj}	F value	Number of samples
Total	Central cities	0.175*** (10.81)	0.9904	0.9890	116.82	80
	Megacities	0.212*** (19.06)	0.9572	0.9511	120.20	240
	Large cities	0.144*** (12.60)	0.9712	0.9671	158.83	624
	Medium-sized cities	0.110*** (10.59)	0.9529	0.9462	112.14	880
	Small and medium-sized cities	0.097*** (4.75)	0.8867	0.8704	22.54	448
Industries	Central cities	0.273*** (12.44)	0.9854	0.9832	154.68	80
	Megacities	0.294*** (11.55)	0.9690	0.9645	133.50	240
	Large cities	0.355*** (14.55)	0.9531	0.9464	211.60	624
	Medium-sized cities	0.231*** (14.59)	0.9571	0.9510	212.79	880
	Small and medium-sized cities	0.225*** (7.36)	0.9338	0.9343	54.16	448
Service industries	Central cities	0.211*** (13.07)	0.9925	0.9914	170.82	80
	Megacities	0.217*** (14.58)	0.9788	0.9757	212.52	240
	Large cities	0.162*** (16.08)	0.9664	0.9616	258.43	624
	Medium-sized cities	0.163*** (16.14)	0.9260	0.9155	260.41	880
	Small and medium-sized cities	0.161*** (10.47)	0.8847	0.8682	109.53	448
Producer service industry	Central cities	0.252*** (14.41)	0.9932	0.9922	207.65	80
	Megacities	0.237*** (10.99)	0.9721	0.9681	120.80	240
	Large cities	0.172*** (10.83)	0.9613	0.9557	117.28	624
	Medium-sized cities	0.151*** (10.18)	0.9283	0.9181	103.65	880
	Small and medium-sized cities	0.143*** (7.96)	0.8739	0.8558	63.36	448

Note: t in parentheses represents "test value". *** indicates significant results at 1% level, ** indicates significant results at 5% level, and * indicates significant results at 10% level. The calculation was completed with the use of measurement software, stata 12.

At the same time, the results show that employment elasticity increases with the development level of cities, indicating that China is still at the stage of industrialisation. Higher level of economic development often means better economic growth with higher pace and the more comprehensive market economy system to create more job opportunities and provide more possibilities for raising income. In this way, big cities become the main channel for absorbing the labor force.

According to industries, large cities have higher employment elasticity in industry. Central cities have begun to shift from a manufacturing centre to a service centre. Megacities and large cities have gradually replaced central cities as new industrial centres, with employment elasticity of 0. 294 and 0. 355. Compared with other industries, industry is still the mainstay of employment in the urban economy, and the employment elasticity in industry is the highest in cities. However, the producer service industry of central cities and megacities have developed rapidly, with employment elasticity of 0.252 and 0. 237 respectively. Although the figures are slightly lower than those in industry (0.273 and 0.294), they are already higher than the overall employment elasticity of service industries (0.211 and 0.217), forming a large gap with other cities. That is to say, central cities and megacities are the main areas for attracting the labor in the producer service industry (see Table 5.1).

Chapter 5.2.2 the Analyses of Labor Relocation

The development of modern cities is the process of continuous construction, deconstruction and reconstruction of industries. In the pre-industrial society, cities often relied on resources or location to become the centre for politics and trade. After entering the era of industrialisation, cities mainly undertook economic functions, industrial companies agglomerated in cities and located around the centre. As the economic intensity increased in urban centres, prices of land, labor and other factors beain to rise, and costs of industrial production increased. In response to the challenge of rising costs, manufacturing companies moved from the central part of cities to those with lower development levels for new agglomeration. Through restructuring the industrial value chain and developing outsourcing business of services, producer service companies replaced manufacturing companies to agglomerate in cities and beame the main driving force for urban economic growth. Urban functions shifted from producing goods and organising to coordinating services as the centre of the economic system.

With the advancement of information technology, the producer service industry can overcome the limitation of location to a certain extent, and serve more producer enterprises in a larger area so that the spatial separability of industries can be fully realised. With the reorganisation of the global economic structure and the promotion of domestic industrial transfer, large cities mainly focus on the service economy, while small and medium-sized cities mainly focus on the industrial economy. Despite the shift of industrial enterprises to the area outside large cities, the development of the producer service industry has effectively avoided the problem of "hollowing out". As the scale of cities expands with higher development levels, the agglomeration of producer service companies can help the larger market to reduce operating costs. In order to be more specialised, in addition to absorbing a large amount of professional labor, producer service companies would also agglomerate for knowledge spillovers. The agglomeration of the producer service industry in cities provides opportunities for the reorganisation of urban industrial structure. The removal of industrial enterprises with high consumption of energy and the agglomeration of producer service industry can help cities form functional clusters. The producer service industry can enhance the position of a city in the global value chain, leading to higher income levels and less environmental and social conflicts.

However, due to information asymmetry, more workers from rural areas seek jobs in cities, making the problem of unemployment more serious, which is the so-called "Todaro Paradox". As the expected return is the main factor of labor mobility, higher income can be earned in cities, while the chance is low for ordinary workers. Due to the restriction of market segmentation, China's urban industries cannot be effectively separated and rationally transferred in accordance with market mechanisms. Industry and service industries locate in cities disorderly. This problem is even more apparent in large cities, leading to a large amount of labor rushing to cities with a series of social problems.

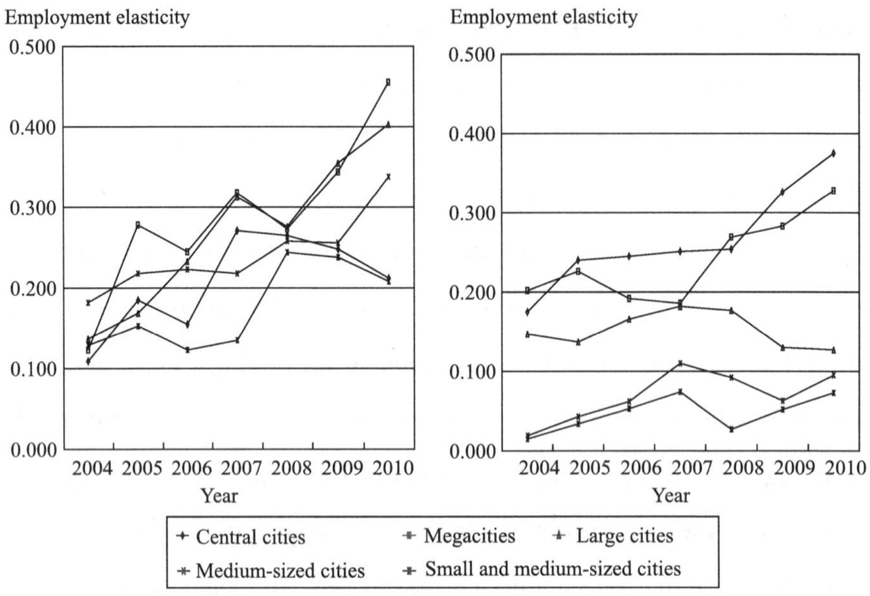

Figure 5.1 Comparison of employment elasticity in industry and the producer service industry in different cities from 2003 to 2010

The non-equilibrium of spatial distribution in economic activities is a typical feature of the real world, and this change is often related to the reorganisation of spatial structure in industries. Only by increasing the degree of freedom in the market economy, we can promote industries to break the limitations of "administrative districts" and rationally reorganise the spatial structure. Producer service companies agglomerate in large cities, and they are more capable than manufacturing companies to pay higher fees for factors of production and use smaller land area. In large cities, due to the scale of the local market, they often have better market opportunities to attract the producer service industry to agglomerate there. The manufacturing industry is moved to other places, due to the outflow of factors, especially labor. City groups form around big cities share a typical "central-periphery" pattern. The spatial distribution of industries is "endogenous". The development of the producer service industry guides the reconstruction of spatial layout, which is conducive to the orderly flow of labor and the transfer between industries. It is also conducive to the improvement of labor productivity while solving urban employment.

According to the changes in employment elasticity, the trend of transforming the industrial structure in the development of the producer service industry in central cities and megacities is becoming increasingly apparent. The employment elasticity of the producer service industry in central cities rose from 0.175 in 2004 to 0.375 in 2010, while the employment elasticity in industry showed a turning point with a downward trend after 2007 (see Figure 5.1). It should be noted that the development of industry in megacities and large cities has attracted more employees, but the employment elasticity of the producer service industry has also shown an upward trend. That is to say, with the development of the economy, the producer service industry is conducive to creating more employment opportunities through industrial linkages. Because central cities stay on the top of the urban pyramid by developing producer services, and more and more industrial enterprises are moving from central cities to megacities or large cities. On the one hand, it reduces operating costs of industrial enterprises in central cities, improves the competitiveness of industrial enterprises, and attracts more industrial workers to transfer to large cities. On the other hand, it also provides more capital and space for central cities to gather more professionals in the producer service industry, optimising the structure of the job market and increasing the capacities of absorbing the labor force in the entire urban system. The employment elasticity in industry of medium-sized cities increases generally, but the employment elasticity of the producer service industry is relatively low. This means that industrial facilities of medium-sized cities support the industrial system of large cities. The employment elasticity in both industry and the producer service industry is low in small and medium-sized cities, showing that the effects of agglomeration in central cities and megacities is greater than those of separate distribution, and the economic functions of small and medium-sized cities are being marginalised.

Chapter 5.2.3 the Analyses of Salaries

The externalisation, marketisation and industrialisation of the producer service industry are the result of specialised division of labor and resource allocation from the inside of enterprises to the market. On the one hand, the internal value chain and industrial chain of enterprises are further specialised, so as to focus on strategic activities and improve the core competitiveness. On the other hand, producer service companies are gradually separated from enterprises to integrate resources and provide high-quality professional services for more enterprises, so the overall economic operational efficiency and competitiveness would be greatly improved. The producer service industry introduces increasingly specialised human resources and intellectual capital into the production process of the manufacturing industry to promote the optimisation, transformation and upgrading of the industrial structure for the high-end position in the value chain and higher profits. With the expansion of the market scale, the producer service industry has absorbed a large amount of specialised labor. More and more workers are engaged in the producer service industry, and the degree of specialisation is getting higher and higher, thereby increasing the overall efficiency of the producer service industry.

The producer service industry has high labor productivity with higher wages, stimulating the supply of specialised labor and increasing the accumulation of human resources through education and training opportunities. The increase inincome level would lead to an increase in the demand of products for additional services, which would promote the demand of industrial products for the producer service industry and drive the further development of the producer service industry. Due to the increased demand, the producer service industry has become more specialised and formed an effective circle. At the same time, the increase in income levels would also cause changes in the structure of consumption. The high-income groups would increase the demand for some consumer services which cannot be traded, thus narrowing the income gap in the process of promoting the overall income level. Most of the workers in producer service companies are highly skilled and professional, so the increase in wages would cause more opportunity costs, thereby increasing the demand for low-skilled workers, such as nannies, cleaners, and nursing staff. Therefore, while increasing the employment rate of cities, it would also promote the income level of low-skilled workers and help narrow the income gap.

Table 5.2 Average wage of employees in different industries in China's urban areas from 2003 to 2010

(Unit: RMB)

Industries \ Year	2003	2004	2005	2006	2007	2008	2009	2010	Average growth (%)
Agriculture, forestry, animal husbandry and fishery	6884	7497	8207	9269	10847	12560	14356	16717	20.41
Mining	13627	16774	20449	24125	28185	34233	38038	44196	32.05
Manufacturing	12671	14251	15934	18225	21144	24404	26810	30916	20.57
Production and supply of electricity, gas and water	18574	21543	24750	28424	33470	38515	41869	47309	22.10
Architecture	11328	12578	14112	16164	18482	21223	24161	27529	20.43
Transportation, warehousing and postal services	15753	18071	20911	24111	27903	32041	35315	40466	22.41
Information transmission, computer services and software	30897	33449	38799	43435	47700	54906	58154	64436	15.51
Wholesale and retail	10894	13012	15256	17796	21074	25818	29139	33635	29.82
Accommodation and catering business	11198	12618	13876	15236	17046	19321	20860	23382	15.54

续表

Industries \ Year	2003	2004	2005	2006	2007	2008	2009	2010	Average growth (%)
Finance	20780	24299	29229	35495	44011	53897	60398	70146	33.94
Real estate	17085	18467	20253	22238	26085	30118	32242	35870	15.71
Leasing and commercial services	17020	18723	21233	24510	27807	32915	35494	39566	18.92
Scientific research, technical services and geological exploration	20442	23351	27155	31644	38432	45512	50143	56376	25.11
Management of water conservancy, environmental and public facilities	11774	12884	14322	15630	18383	21103	23159	25544	16.71
Resident services and other services	12665	13680	15747	18030	20370	22858	25172	28206	17.53
Education	14189	16085	18259	20918	25908	29831	34543	38968	24.95
Healthcare and social welfare	16185	18386	20808	23590	27892	32185	35662	40232	21.23
Culture, sports and entertainment	17098	20522	22670	25847	30430	34158	37755	41428	20.33
Public administration and social organisations	15355	17372	20234	22546	27731	32296	35326	38242	21.29
Average	13969	15920	18200	20856	24721	28898	32244	36539	23.08

Source: Department of National Accounts, National Bureau of Statistics. China Statistical Yearbook (2010). China Statistics Press, 2011.

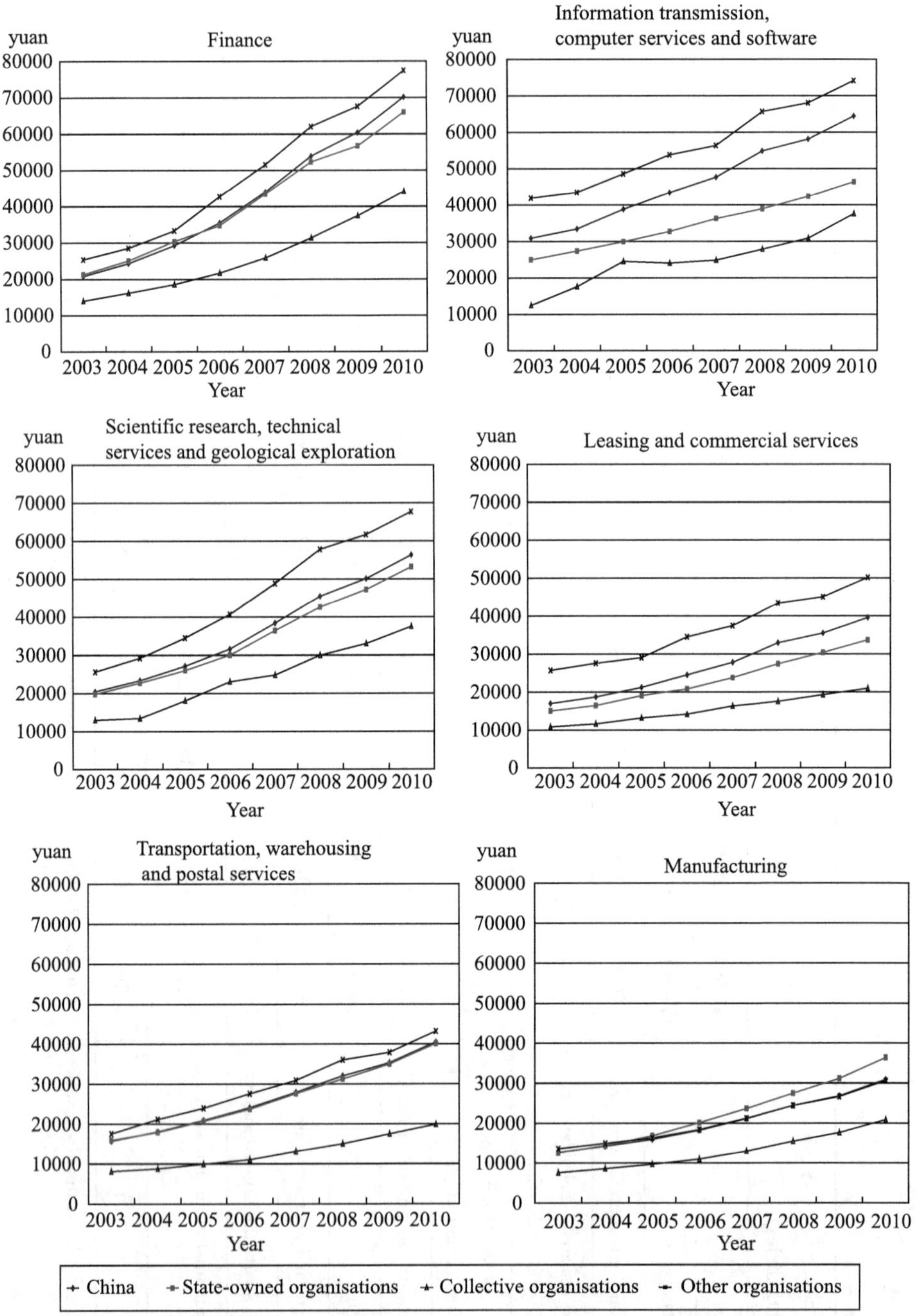

Finance

Information transmission, computer services and software

Scientific research, technical services and geological exploration

Leasing and commercial services

Transportation, warehousing and postal services

Manufacturing

China · State-owned organisations · Collective organisations · Other organisations

Figure 5.2 Average wages of employees in manufacturing and producer service industries in urban areas from 2003 to 2010

From 2003 to 2010, the three areas with the highest average annual wages in urban organisations would be finance(RMB 70146), information transmission, computing services and software (RMB 64436), scientific research, technical services and geological exploration(RMB 56376)in the producer service industry.In addition, the average wages in the areas of transportation,warehousing and postal services(RMB 40466), leasing and business services (RMB 39566) were much higher than that of the manufacturing industry (RMB 309116) (see Table 5.2).Manufacturing has gradually become a typical part with low profits,and profits have begun to shift from the process of producing goods to the producer services of finance, information, scientific research,logistics and commerce.The transfer of the receiaer & creator of the value can help improve the wage level in the producer service industry.From another perspective,developing all services and auxiliary activities involved in the value chain is conducive to enhancing the capabilities of conducting independent research and development for enterprises and the degree of specialised division of labor within enterprises, so as to promote the transformation and upgrading of industries.

Chapter 5.3 The Summary

With the adjustment of the urban industrial structure,the key role of the producer service industry in promoting the optimisation of the employment structure is mainly reflected in the following aspects. ①With the improvement of economic development and the increasingly specialised division of labor, dividing and reorganising the industrial value chain would further increase the demand for producer services and the employment rate of professional labor. At the same time, through industrial linkages, the producer service industry would also increase the employment rate of other industries, expanding the total employment rate and quality of services eventually. ② In the process of industrialisation, the urban system of division of labor centring around central cities of Beijing, Shanghai and Guangzhou is under construction, and the producer service industry is concentrated in central cities and megacities. Large cities become new industrial centres, and a large number of medium-sized cities develop functional facilities to support megacities and large cities. The gradual improvement of the urban system is also the process of promoting the orderly flow of labor and solving structural contradictions in the employment market. ③ As the producer service industry is at the high end of the value chain and labor productivity is higher, so there are higher wages. Changes in the consumption structure and the increase in consumption would also lead to an increase in the income level of other industries, which narrows the income gap between cities and industries to a certain extent.

In order to further benefit from the producer service industry in promoting the optimisation of employment structure in urban areas, it is necessary to support with policies. The first is to guide the industrial transfer through environmental rules and policies, promote the division of the industrial value chain and formulation of related policies, and encourage the development of the producer service industry in a broader area, so as to improve the capacities of absorbing the labor force and the orderly flow of labor. The problem that "expenditure is controlled by pollution" is caused by environmental regulations, and it would increase the production costs of industrial enterprises in urban areas to reduce the scale of production or move to cities with larger ecological capacities. This can help companies transfer and upgrade for environmental protection so that industrial workers can be optimally deployed in the urban system. At the same time, industrial enterprises with heavy emission of pollutants can also consider environmental regulations a competitive factor. The producer service industry can help industrial enterprises to obtain comparative advantages, reduce dependence on resources and bring employment growth. Therefore, developing the producer service industry can help "double dividends" of energy conservation, reduction in emitting pollutants and employment growth through environmental regulations (Lu, 2011). [96]

The second is to further standardise the market mechanism and create conditions for the agglomeration of producer service companies in central cities and megacities. The market segmentation and household registration system caused by the economy based on "administrative districts" have restricted the urban expansion and free flow of labor for the long term, and it cannot give full play to economies of scale in cities and the specialisation of the urban system. The expansion of urban scale, especially in megacities, can increase the employment rate of the entire city. Workers with higher and lower degree of specialisation can enjoy more benefits, which is also conducive to the realisation of inclusive growth (Lu et al., 2012).[97] Giving full play to the role of market mechanisms, reducing administrative interventions by the government and creating conditions for the orderly flow of labor can be beneficial to optimising allocation of resources and structure of job market. It is also conducive to accumulating human resources in the process of transfer, so as to improve the competitiveness of enterprises and cities.

The third is to accelerate the institutional reform of service industries. Since producer service companies are mostly small and medium-sized, the past state-owned institutional constraints cannot be applied to the development of enterprises under the rapid improvement of modern new technologies. In the traditional industries like finance, communication and transportation, the market monopoly has been formed for high profits. This market structure is not conducive to the competition of the producer service industry, and it would also increase the cost of producer services in the manufacturing industry, resulting in inefficiency of the entire economy. Therefore, allowing private and foreign enterprises to enter in a broader area would invite the competition and vitalise the development of the producer service industry.

Chapter Six

Impacts of Developing the Producer Service Industry on "Dematerialisation"

The global economic competition is largely reflected by comparing economic development levels in cities. Although China's urbanisation has been advancing quickly, however, in the process of development of China's cities, "urban diseases" are becoming more and more prominent, such as overpopulation, environmental pollution and resource shortages. There would be further restraints on resources and the environment, weakening competitiveness in cities. With the promotion of globalisation and information technology, the producer service industry has become the main driving force for economic growth. It would also alleviate pressure from resources and the environment through the process of "dematerialisation".

Chapter 6.1 The Kuznets Curve and Targets of "Dematerialisation"

The traditional extensive economic development pattern pursues economic growth, constantly transforming a large amount of natural resources into man-made capital. A lot of investment in more material resources is made to produce more wealth to meet human needs. "Dematerialisation" emphasises that we must ensure the stability of natural capital stock and make artificial capital provide more utility at the same time, which is an inevitable requirement for the intensive development of modern economy. The so-called "dematerialisation" is the absolute (or relative) reduction in the amount of materials consumed or waste generated by human economic and social development when satisfying basic needs. That is, while pursuing goals for economic growth, we strive to minimise environmental stress. We should promote the use of a certain amount of material resources to create more utility for human needs rather than more material products. "Dematerialisation" is an important part of strategies for economic sustainable development, which proposes a new way to resolve the contradiction between resource shortages and environmental pollution

(Wang & Li, 2010).[98] In the most well-known concept of "dematerialisation", the overall goal should be the figure of 4 times, requiring the productivity of natural resources to increase through reducing material input by half and doubling the income or output within 50 years in order to guarantee the carrying capacity of the ecosystem(von Weizsäcker, 1997).[99] At present, China is still at the stage of industrialisation, and economic growth mainly depends on the heavy consumption of natural resources. It is the general trend of urban development to transform the economic development pattern for sustainability, reduce and eliminate negative impacts of social and economic development on the environment and promote "dematerialisation" (Pan & Fu, 2008).[100] At the 2009 United Nations Climate Conference in Copenhagen, China made a commitment to the world: our energy consumption for the gross domestic product in 2020 would be 40-45% lower than that in 2005.

"Dematerialisation" includes the reduction of material resources inputted into the economic system from the ecological system, in case the consumption of resources is faster than the regeneration rate of resources, to help the degradation of the ecological system. It also includes the reduction of the amount of waste discharged from the economic system into the environment so that the amount of pollutants does not exceed the carrying capacity of the environment to prevent serious pollution. Therefore, "dematerialisation" is the reduction of materials at both ends of the production, which changes the low efficiency management of the environment from the end of production in the past and makes the operation of the economic system more sustainable. "Dematerialisation" means reducing the amount of material input from the economic system and the amount of waste discharged into the ecological system to ultimately separate economic growth from environmental degradation and pollution. "Dematerialisation" is divided into "relative dematerialisation" and "absolute dematerialisation" (Clevel & Ruth, 1999).[101] During a certain period of time, when the growth rate of material consumption or pollutant emissions is lower than the rate of economic growth, it is called "relative dematerialisation", which refers to the relative reduction in material consumption. That is to say, materials are used less intensively with higher utilisation efficiency, reflecting positive effects from technological advancement and the promotion of economies of scale on "dematerialisation". However, the "relative dematerialisation" achieved by technological advancement and economies of scale may also lead to a sharp increase in consumption and an increase in the total consumption of materials, which is known as the "rebound effect". As the economy continues to grow, the amount of material consumption and pollutant emissions reduces gradually, which is called "absolute dematerialisation", which refers to the absolute reduction in material consumption, and it is a key factor in measuring sustainable development.

In 1993, Panayotou (1993) used Kuznets' method of measuring the inequality between economic development level and income by the inverted "U" curve, and described the relationship between environmental quality and economic development level as the

"Environmental Kuznets Curve" for the first time.[102] At the early stage of economic development, income per capita is relatively low, and material needs and environmental pressure would be relatively small as well. During the era of industrialisation, the economy grows rapidly, the number of material products increases significantly to meet the demand for better living conditions after the increase in income levels. At this time, the quantity demanded of materials and consumption reach a peak, and the environmental deterioration would climb to the highest point gradually. With the completion of industrialisation, the increase in income level would lead to the structural transformation from consuming products themselves to enjoying functional services of products, which reduces the intensive usage of materials and improves the environment. Therefore, with the improvement of the economic development, the changes in environmental quality or demand for goods show the inverted "U" curve, so the hypothesis of the Environmental Kuznets Curve is also applicable to the process of "dematerialisation" (Bartelmus, 2008).[103] According to data published by "the World Energy Outlook of the International Energy Agency", China consumed the amount of energy which was equivalent to 2.25 billion tons of oil in 2010, surpassing the United States to become the country with the largest consumption of energy in the world.[104] China's industrial consumption of energy accounted for 70% of the total consumption, due to the large proportion of heavy industries with high energy consumption in China, such as steel and cement industries. However, the main reason for the huge gap in energy consumption for the gross domestic product between

China and the United States is not industry but service industries. Service industries with low energy consumption contributed $ 11.2 trillion to the gross domestic product in the United States, accounting for 79% of the gross domestic product. China's service industries only made US $ 2.2 trillion, which was less than one fifth of that in the United States. In addition to the relatively high energy consumption in the fields of logistics and transportation, most service industries consume very little energy. Therefore, we must change the pattern of economic development and reduce the energy consumption per unit of the gross domestic product in China. The key is to develop service industries, especially technology-intensive and knowledge-intensive technical services and business services in the producer service industry. This is the best way to achieve economic "dematerialisation" and an important prerequisite for the Environmental Kuznets Curve.

The producer service industry provides professional services and runs through the entire production process. With the development of the economy, the market has been continuously expanded, the specialised division of labor has been gradually deepened, and the production process has become more and more roundabout. A more roundabout production process requires more professional and diverse intermediate inputs. Through putting two advanced factors of production, namely intellectual capital and human resources, producer service enterprises can promote production to be more roundabout and specialised with deepening investment of capital. It can also improve the productivity of labor and other factors of production, and the expansion of the scale reduces production costs of products, directly improving production efficiency and industrial competitiveness. Buying producer services is not for final consumption, but intermediate investment for production to create greater value. Therefore, the input of producer services is essentially an alternative to material inputs, so as to achieve technological progress and economies of scale through the division of labor for higher economic growth efficiency. Under the condition of not increasing or even reducing material input, increasing the intermediate input of producer services can improve production efficiency and reduce material consumption to produce products and achieve the goal of "dematerialisation".

The producer service industry provides services for the production process, and the intermediate investment is the essential industrial feature. The input-output method can be used to separate the intermediate use and the final consumption of service industries to properly distinguish the intermediate use of services (producer service) and the final use of services. It can also effectively overcome the one-sidedness caused by dividing the producer service industry according to certain subjective standards, so as to accurately reflect the situation of the producer service industry and impacts on "dematerialisation". Therefore, this book uses the input-output method to comprehensively analyse impacts of the producer service industry on economic growth and "dematerialisation".

Chapter 6.2 The Input-Output Table and Analysis of Indicators

The input-output method was proposed by Leontief in 1936. With the use of a matrix, it describes the source of input and the use of output in production activities of various sectors in the national economy during a certain period, so as to reveal the relationship between various sectors of the national economy that are interdependent and mutually constrained. [105] The relationship is: intermediate use + final consumption − import + others = total output; intermediate input + added value = total input; total input = total output. The proportion that a department uses intermediate inputs from various sectors to the total output (or total input) is called the direct consumption coefficient. The complete consumption coefficient reflects the consumption and dependence between departments in the production cycle, which is the sum of direct consumption and various indirect consumption. For individual sectors and the national economy, the relationship of intermediate use (X), direct consumption coefficient (A), the Leontief inverse matrix (B) and complete consumption coefficient (C) is shown below:

$$X=(X_{ij})_{n\times n} \tag{6.1}$$

$$A=(a_{ij})_{n\times n},a_{ij}=X_{ij}/\sum_{j}X_{ij} \tag{6.2}$$

$$B=(b_{ij})_{n\times n}=(I-A)^{-1} \tag{6.3}$$

$$C=(c_{ij})_{n\times n}=B-A \tag{6.4}$$
$$(i=1,2,\cdots,n;j=1,2,\cdots,n)$$

X_{ij} represents the intermediate input of the industry i used for the output of the industry j . a_{ij} , b_{ij} and c_{ij} represent the direct consumption coefficient, the coefficient of the Leontief inverse matrix, and the complete consumption coefficient respectively. In addition, this book also uses the following indicators for analysis:

(1) The first would be the material input rate and the service input rate. The intermediate inputs of various industries or sectors in the national economy are divided into material inputs and service inputs, and service inputs are producer services. The material input rate refers to the proportion of material inputs of various industries or sectors in the national economy to the total input (or total output), reflecting the degree of material dependence that output growth has in various sectors of the national economy. The service input rate refers to the proportion of service inputs of various industries or sectors in the national economy to the total input (or total output), reflecting the level of providing services in various sectors of the national economy.

(2) The second would be the structure of service input and usage. In the total output of the service industry, part of the output is used for intermediate inputs, the rest is used for final consumption, and the part for intermediate inputs would be producer services. The structure of service input refers to the proportion of services inputted by various industries or sectors in the national economy to the intermediate input of service industries, reflecting which industries or sectors use producer

services. The structure of service usage refers to the proportion of services use used by various industries or sectors in the national economy to the intermediate use of the industries or sectors, reflecting the use of producer services the industries or sectors.

(3) The third would be the industrial correlation coefficient. The industrial correlation coefficient includes the influence coefficient and the response coefficient. The former reflects the extent to which the demand generated and influences on other sectors of the national economy when a sector increases a unit of final consumption. The latter reflects the response in a sector when various sectors increases a unit of final consumption in the national economy, that is, the amount of output that this sector needs to produce for others. The equations for calculating the influence coefficient (F_j) and the response coefficient (E_i) are shown below:

$$F_j = \sum_{i=1}^{n} b_{ij} / \frac{1}{n} \sum_{i=1}^{n} \sum_{j=1}^{n} b_{ij} \ ; \ E_i = \sum_{j=1}^{n} b_{ij} / \frac{1}{n} \sum_{i=1}^{n} \sum_{j=1}^{n} b_{ij} \qquad (6.5)$$

$$(i=1,2,\cdots,n;j=1,2,\cdots,n)$$

b_{ij} is the coefficient of the Leontief inverse matrix. The influence coefficient $F_j > 1$ indicates that the sector j has greater impacts on the national economy than the average influencing power of other sectors. The larger the value of F_j , the greater impacts the sector j has on the national economy. The response coefficient $E_i > 1$ indicates that the sector i is more responsive to the national economy than the average level of sectors. The larger the value of E_i , the greater impacts the national economy has on the sector i .

Chapter 6.3 Empirical Analyses of Impacts of the Producer Service Industry on "Dematerialisation" in Urban Economy

The input-output method analysis can comprehensively reflect the effects of the intermediate input of producer services on the national economy, so as to describe the process of "dematerialisation" scientifically. Changes in service input rates and material input rates reflect changes in service inputs and material inputs during the production process, which would be the degree of providing services and "dematerialisation" in the national economy. Changing the quality and structure of inputs is also the reflection of technological progress. The structure of service input shows the contribution of the producer service industry to the "dematerialisation" of various sectors in the national economy. The structure of service usage reflects the degree of providing services in the production process of various sectors in the national economy. The industrial correlation coefficient reflects the promotion of economic growth by the producer service industry and the impacts of economic growth on the producer service industry. That is to say, "dematerialisation" happens in the process of economic growth.

In the empirical analysis, this book selects the input-output tables from 42 sectors for 2002, 2005 and 2007 in four cities directly under the Central Government, including Beijing, Tianjin, Shanghai and Chongqing (collected from the Input-Output Table in China written by "the Department of National Accounts of the National Bureau of Statistics in 2002, 2005, and 2007"). This book studies the impacts of developing the producer service industry in four cities in different regions and at different stages of economic development on the process of "dematerialisation" in urban economy. Only cities directly under the Central Government in China have a relatively continuous and comprehensive input-output tables, and they are located in three different regions, including the northern, eastern and southwest areas of China. The level of economic development is not the same in these four cities, and they have different patterns for the transformation of industrial structure, making it representative relatively.

Chapter 6.3.1 Analyses of Service Input Rate and Material Input Rate

By calculating the service input rate and material input rate of Beijing, Tianjin, Shanghai and Chongqing in 2002, 2005 and 2007, we can find different cities showed different trends (see Table 6.1). According to the service input rate, the rate in Beijing increased year by year, the rate in Shanghai stabilised after rising, the rate in Tianjin stabilised after decline, and that of Chongqing declined year by year. The material input rate showed the opposite trend. The change in service input rate or material input rate would be related to the stage of urban economic development. Beijing was entering the post-industrial era, and the proportion of service economy was as high as 72.1%. Shanghai's service industries also surpassed the secondary industry and reached

52.6% at the later stage of industrialisation that constructed the industrial structure in accordance with the importance of developing tertiary sector, secondary sector, and primary sector. The service input rate in Tianjin and Chongqing both showed a downward trend, mainly because the industrialisation of these two cities was still advancing. The proportion of the secondary industry was relatively high, and the economic growth mainly depended on the secondary industry with high material input.

According to production efficiency, the input-output ratio of service industries was about three times higher than that of the secondary industry in four cities. This reflected that the gross domestic product per capita in cities with a high proportion of service industries would be correspondingly higher. The gross domestic product per capita of Shanghai, Beijing, and Tianjin in 2007 was 3.99, 3.50, and 2.44 times higher than that of Chongqing respectively. According to the rules of transforming the industrial structure, the development of producer service industry applies the trend of urban economic transformation from a "manufacturing centre" to "service centre". Improving the service input rate in the production process and the quality of the intermediate input is an important way to strengthen the economic growth effectively and help reduce the material input and energy consumption of the production process.

Table 6. 1 Comparing the rate of intermediate input, input-output ratio and level of economic growth in Beijing, Tianjin, Shanghai and Chongqin in 2002, 2005 and 2007

Cities	Year	Rate of intermediate input (%)		Input-output ratio		Gross domestic product per capita (RMB)	Total gross domestic product (RMB in trillion)	Proportion of t hree industries (%)
		Rate of service input	Rate of material input	Secondary industry	Tertiary industry			
Beijing	2002	26. 49	35. 82	1: 0. 33	1 : 0. 96	27746	3212. 71	3. 1 : 35. 6 : 61. 3
	2005	30. 35	36. 55	1 : 0. 28	1 : 0. 75	45444	6886. 31	1. 4 : 29. 5 : 69. 1
	2007	31. 21	32. 98	1 : 0. 29	1 : 0. 84	58204	9353. 32	1. 1 : 26. 8 : 72. 1
Tianjin	2002	17. 72	50. 06	1 : 0. 33	1 : 0. 85	22068	2051. 16	4. 1 : 48. 4 : 47. 5
	2005	10. 91	57. 63	1 : 0. 31	1 : 1. 20	35785	3697. 62	3. 0 : 55. 5 : 41. 5
	2007	11. 67	56. 36	1 : 0. 33	1 : 1. 11	46122	5050. 40	2. 2 : 57. 3 : 40. 5
Shanghai	2002	17. 56	50. 15	1 : 0. 31	1 : 0. 94	40524	5408. 76	1. 6 : 47. 4 : 51. 0
	2005	20. 60	49. 59	1 : 0. 29	1 : 0. 73	51474	9154. 18	0. 9 : 48. 6 : 50. 5
	2007	19. 40	52. 44	1 : 0. 25	1 : 0. 76	66367	12188. 85	0. 8 : 46. 6 : 52. 6
Chongqing	2002	16. 62	47. 41	1 : 0. 34	1 : 0. 90	7912	2232. 86	14. 2 : 42. 9 : 42. 9
	2005	13. 17	46. 37	1 : 0. 38	1 : 1. 35	12404	3467. 72	13. 4 : 45. 1 : 41. 5
	2007	11. 29	50. 92	1 : 0. 38	1 : 1. 33	16629	4676. 13	10. 3 : 50. 7 : 39. 0

Chapter 6.3.2 Analyses of Industrial Structure and Functional Layout of the Producer Service Industry

The producer service industry needs to play a major role in the process of "dematerialisation" in the national economy, and the key is to realise the effective integration with the production process. At the stage of industrialisation, the producer service industry mainly serves the secondary industry, especially the manufacturing industry, which plays an important role in industrial upgrading. After entering the post-industrial society, the manufacturing industry provides more services gradually, and the producer service industry is mainly invested in the tertiary industry. According to the structure of input, the producer service industry mainly serves the tertiary industry (except Chongqing), but it does not mean that China has fully entered the post-industrial society. As the market reform of China's producer service industry is relatively lagging behind, the degree of industrial agglomeration is relatively high. Typical areas of the producer service industry, such as telecommunication and finance, have been in monopolistic competition for the long run, strengthening the "internalisation of services" in producer service enterprises. This also highlights the low level of manufacturing development that has led to insufficient demand for external producer services. With the advancement of marketisation and industrialisation, the proportion of producer services to the tertiary industry tends to decline, but the proportion of producer services to the secondary industry rises constantly(except for the slight increase in Shanghai in 2007).It shows that the development of China's urban producer service industry mainly concentrates on the in-depth promotion of industrialisation for a long time in the future(see Table 6.2).Changes in the structure of input in the producer service industry are caused by structural changes in the production system. Only when the level of economic development leads to changes in the structure of consumer demand, can more producer services be invested in service industries instead of the manufacturing industry.

According to the structure of usage, the proportion of producer services used by the primary industry is relatively small with an upward trend. This is the result of the gradual marketisation of agriculture, leading to higher demand for producer services, such as research and development, finance and market services. The use of producer services in the secondary industry is consistent with the level of industrialisation. The year-on-year rise in Beijing is consistent with the highly developed manufacturing industry. Tianjin and Shanghai maintain a relative balanced transformation of industrial structure. The year-on-year decline in Chongqing reflects that the development of the manufacturing industry has not increased the demand for producer services, but raised the dependence on materials and resources. The use of producer services in the tertiary industry varies in cities with different economic development levels. The tertiary industry in Beijing and Shanghai tends to use a relatively large proportion of producer services. A well-functioning internal cycle has been basically formed in fields of modern producer services, such as science and technology, and business services. The decline in the use of producer services by the tertiary industry in Tianjin and Chongqing is caused by the overlarge proportion of traditional producer services, such as transportation, wholesale and retail, and the consumption of materials and energy is relatively high. Compared with Beijing, there is still large potential for the use of producer services in various industries in Tianjin, Shanghai and Chongqing. The key is to change the concept of relying on resources to drive economic growth, and strive to adjust the industrial structure for sustainable economic development and stimulate the demand of the production system for the producer service industry.

Table 6.2 Ratio of input and usage in the producer service industry in Beijing, Tianjin, Shanghai and Chongqing in 2002, 2005 and 2007

%

Industries \ Year \ City		Beijing			Tianjin			Shanghai			Chongqing		
		2002	2005	2007	2002	2005	2007	2002	2005	2007	2002	2005	2007
Structure of input	Primary industry	0.43	0.19	1.47	1.09	0.96	0.79	1.21	0.27	0.99	1.32	2.96	3.95
	Secondary industry	35.21	42.47	43.83	40.02	41.94	45.71	39.41	55.35	35.04	44.09	48.58	49.04
	Tertiary industry	64.36	57.24	54.99	59.35	56.86	53.49	59.38	44.37	63.97	54.59	48.46	47.01
Structure of usage	Primary industry	8.90	11.67	27.32	10.95	12.05	10.12	14.11	11.90	34.54	7.52	10.59	15.16
	Secondary industry	25.78	32.78	33.99	15.35	9.20	11.39	14.70	21.57	14.03	15.94	14.92	11.62
	Tertiary industry	68.58	64.78	75.98	51.15	34.99	30.81	54.49	54.21	54.38	60.42	49.23	45.68

Source: Department of National Accounts, National Bureau of Statistics. Input-Output Table in China. China Statistics Press, 2012.

Chapter 6.3.3 Analyses of Industrial Linkages

When the influence coefficient is greater than 1, it means that the sector plays a vital role in the national economy. China is still in the process of comprehensive industrialisation. The economic growth of the four cities is mainly driven by manufacturing. In the tertiary industry, traditional sectors are the main part in the producer service sector that the influence coefficient is greater than 1, such as tourism (Beijing, Shanghai and Chongqing have rich resources of tourism), transportation and warehousing (Tianjin and Shanghai are important ports). The modern sectors occupy a relatively small proportion. The influence coefficient is greater than 1 only in the areas of information transmission, computing services and software, and scientific research in Beijing, and leasing and business services in Shanghai and Chongqing (see Table 6.3). In cities with relatively developed economies like Beijing and Shanghai, the role of modern producer services becomes more and more important in the economy, while the traditional producer services in Tianjin and Chongqing have a relatively large role in driving the economy.

When the response coefficient is greater than 1, the sector is greatly affected by the national economy. With the rapid development of China's economy, the demand for the producer service industry has increased largely. Producer services are mainly transportation and warehousing, wholesale and retail, financial insurance, leasing and business services, which play an auxiliary role in the production process. The economic growth is supported by high-tech services, such as information transmission, computing services and software, scientific research, and comprehensive technical services, but the demand for these services is relatively small. This is determined by the extensive growth pattern of China's urban economy. Economic growth relies on the increase of material input and economies of scale to produce large quantities of cheap industrial products with low added value, and the task of "dematerialisation" is urgent and hard to achieve.

Chapter 6.3.4 Analyses of Division in the Producer Service Industry

The producer service industry is usually divided into the traditional producer service industry and the modern producer service industry. The traditional producer service industry mainly provides services for logistics and financial institutions, including transportation and warehousing, wholesale and retail, and finance and insurance. Enterprises in the traditional producer service industry mainly improve the efficiency of the production process through economies of scale on the basis of dividing the industrial chain. They aim to increase the efficiency of material use in the production process. The modern producer service industry primarily provides services for the fields of information, technology and management, including information technology and computing, science and technology, leasing and business. Enterprises in the modern producer service industry are relatively small in scale, but they provide highly customised services through putting intellectual capital and human resources into the production process. The purpose is to reduce the material input in the production process by replacing it with services.

China is still in the period of industrialisation. The producer service industry mainly provides auxiliary services for industrial production, and the main components are still traditional producer services, such as transportation and warehousing, as well as wholesale and retail. The proportion of Tianjin and Chongqing is about 50%, which is about 10% higher than that of Beijing and Shanghai (see Table 6.4). In the most developed cities in China like Beijing and Shanghai, the financial and insurance industry would be the most important sector of the producer service industry, accounting for about 20% of the total service industries. It should be pointed out that the modern producer service industry is also developing rapidly in Beijing and Shanghai. As Beijing relies on its unique advantages of talents and technology, the proportion of information transmission and computing services, scientific research and technical services has increased year by year to become the most important centre for research and development. Shanghai makes full use of its central position in the Yangtze River Delta and the high degree of dependence on foreign trade to intensively develop business services and build an important base for international outsourcing business of services. Therefore, Tianjin and Chongqing should develop the traditional producer service industry around the upgrading of industrialisation, reduce the material dependence in the production process, and improve the material consumption of products for new industrialisation. Beijing and Shanghai should focus on economic transformation of cities to develop modern producer services, like research and development, design and business services at the high end of the industrial chain, so as to improve the added value of services and the benefits of economic growth in the production process.

Table 6. 3 Influence coefficient and response coefficient of the producer service industry in Beijing, Tianjin, Shanghai and Chongqing in 2002, 2005 and 2007

Industries \ City / Year		Beijing			Tianjin			Shanghai			Chongqing	
		2002	2005	2007	2002	2005	2007	2002	2005	2007	2005	2007
Influence coefficient	Transportation and warehousing	0. 944	1. 028	0. 874	0. 841	1. 058	1. 189	1. 135	1. 159	1. 168	0. 935	0. 778
	Postal services	0. 798	0. 681	0. 623	0. 651	0. 877	1. 182	0. 765	0. 766	0. 718	0. 927	0. 896
	Information transmission, computer services and software	0. 863	1. 066	1. 089	0. 535	0. 468	0. 567	0. 781	1. 000	0. 867	0. 699	0. 719
	Wholesale and retail	0. 603	0. 729	0. 616	1. 167	0. 414	0. 420	0. 638	0. 826	0. 445	0. 490	0. 551
	Accommodation and catering business	0. 863	0. 980	0. 803	1. 023	0. 934	0. 842	1. 028	1. 162	1. 096	1. 002	0. 961
	Financial insurance	0. 685	0. 375	0. 431	0. 767	0. 391	0. 268	0. 574	0. 331	0. 728	0. 609	0. 623
	Real estate	0. 840	0. 494	0. 405	0. 727	0. 424	0. 237	0. 448	0. 564	0. 705	0. 298	0. 293
	Leasing and commercial services	0. 666	1. 095	0. 989	0. 670	1. 086	0. 910	1. 047	1. 316	1. 226	1. 331	1. 076
	Tourism	0. 703	1. 456	1. 080	0. 600	0. 601	0. 941	1. 418	1. 776	1. 029	0. 842	1. 162
	Scientific research	0. 835	0. 977	1. 184	0. 537	0. 952	0. 861	0. 899	0. 844	1. 149	1. 171	0. 985
	Comprehensive technical services	0. 882	1. 205	0. 872	0. 592	0. 868	0. 443	1. 176	1. 098	0. 964	0. 777	0. 484
	Other social services	0. 829	1. 197	1. 114	1. 013	1. 056	0. 874	0. 951	1. 144	1. 065	0. 781	0. 783
	Education	0. 738	0. 552	0. 681	0. 513	0. 469	0. 510	0. 515	0. 627	0. 474	0. 312	0. 590
	Healthcare and social welfare	1. 040	1. 042	0. 978	0. 801	1. 061	1. 051	0. 984	1. 055	1. 115	0. 895	0. 884
	Culture, sports and entertainment	0. 799	0. 974	0. 886	0. 427	1. 116	1. 006	0. 978	0. 960	0. 912	0. 936	0. 797
	Public administration and social organisations	0. 822	0. 822	0. 749	0. 554	0. 531	0. 556	0. 874	0. 955	0. 945	0. 830	0. 748

续表

	Industries \ City / Year	Beijing			Tianjin			Shanghai			Chongqing	
		2002	2005	2007	2002	2005	2007	2002	2005	2007	2005	2007
Response coefficient	Transportation and warehousing	1. 988	2. 549	2. 998	3. 399	3. 684	5. 204	2. 646	1. 252	2. 482	2. 367	2. 106
	Postal services	0. 146	0. 235	0. 037	0. 091	0. 088	0. 103	0. 070	0. 038	0. 038	0. 027	0. 135
	Information transmission, computer services and software	1. 308	2. 044	0. 471	0. 405	0. 637	0. 310	0. 912	1. 111	3. 032	0. 502	0. 273
	Wholesale and retail	0. 452	1. 078	2. 330	2. 655	2. 305	2. 502	2. 851	1. 826	2. 185	0. 389	1. 594
	Accommodation and catering business	0. 660	0. 851	0. 692	0. 630	0. 476	0. 819	0. 443	0. 413	0. 299	0. 727	0. 927
	Financial insurance	2. 945	1. 824	0. 983	1. 843	1. 662	1. 669	2. 488	0. 641	2. 253	2. 359	1. 575
	Real estate	1. 083	0. 126	0. 346	0. 491	0. 741	0. 615	0. 737	0. 657	0. 591	0. 245	0. 221
	Leasing and commercial services	2. 324	1. 847	1. 510	1. 253	0. 787	1. 358	0. 975	2. 510	2. 737	1. 143	0. 565
	Tourism	0. 017	0. 178	0. 328	0. 025	0. 015	0. 091	0. 133	0. 380	0. 106	0. 004	0. 051
	Scientific research	0. 481	0. 260	0. 678	0. 565	0. 622	0. 105	0. 174	0. 151	0. 392	0. 513	0. 145
	Comprehensive technical services	1. 447	2. 103	0. 160	0. 036	0. 082	0. 184	0. 555	0. 945	0. 047	0. 074	0. 368
	Other social services	0. 309	0. 996	0. 240	0. 913	0. 904	0. 379	0. 232	0. 352	0. 077	0. 406	0. 248
	Other social services	0. 117	0. 246	0. 109	0. 066	0. 070	0. 136	0. 051	0. 055	0. 043	0. 112	0. 138
	Healthcare and social welfare	0. 155	0. 041	0. 006	0. 590	0. 602	0. 187	0. 068	0. 077	0. 010	0. 126	0. 274
	Culture, sports and entertainment	0. 726	0. 515	0. 410	0. 202	0. 200	0. 192	0. 389	0. 174	0. 151	0. 278	0. 080
	Public administration and social organisations	0. 017	0. 029	0. 054	0. 000	0. 000	0. 009	0. 014	0. 014	0. 010	0. 075	0. 029

Source: Department of National Accounts, National Bureau of Statistics. Input–Output Table in China. China Statistics Press, 2012.

Table 6. 4 Composition of the producer service industry in Beijing, Tianjin and Shanghai in 2002, 2005 and 2007 %

Industries \ City / Year	Beijing			Tianjin			Shanghai			Chongqing	
	2002	2005	2007	2002	2005	2007	2002	2005	2007	2005	2007
Transportation and warehousing	6. 45	7. 55	7. 71	20. 62	14. 44	14. 05	10. 03	11. 93	10. 59	15. 91	15. 77
Postal services	0. 56	0. 94	0. 61	0. 49	0. 36	0. 31	0. 65	0. 48	0. 46	0. 33	0. 35
Information transmission, computer services and software	12. 77	12. 24	12. 98	5. 06	5. 03	4. 53	6. 81	7. 65	8. 09	6. 36	7. 16
Wholesale and retail	8. 87	13. 72	12. 40	16. 84	28. 43	24. 35	19. 23	17. 92	17. 46	20. 60	22. 08
Accommodation and catering business	3. 95	3. 84	4. 37	4. 28	4. 57	4. 52	5. 03	3. 60	2. 82	4. 94	5. 52
Financial insurance	18. 34	17. 55	18. 19	7. 59	10. 38	14. 07	21. 25	15. 26	17. 86	6. 90	7. 38
Real estate	8. 21	9. 55	11. 86	10. 14	8. 39	9. 25	13. 58	14. 41	11. 53	10. 67	7. 53
Leasing and commercial services	12. 29	7. 14	5. 74	5. 22	2. 55	3. 42	2. 79	6. 60	9. 60	1. 69	2. 37
Tourism	0. 32	0. 14	2. 36	0. 09	0. 43	0. 74	0. 40	0. 16	1. 03	0. 74	0. 36
Scientific research	3. 69	2. 43	6. 62	0. 79	0. 66	4. 71	1. 36	1. 20	3. 12	0. 29	1. 77
Comprehensive technical services	8. 41	4. 96	0. 95	3. 57	4. 85	1. 72	1. 38	3. 44	0. 94	2. 58	2. 38
Other social services	1. 54	2. 50	0. 85	4. 69	5. 42	4. 06	2. 05	2. 83	2. 42	4. 53	3. 09
Education	4. 30	6. 61	4. 64	8. 36	6. 08	5. 92	5. 26	5. 78	5. 74	9. 91	8. 37
Healthcare and social welfare	1. 54	2. 44	2. 81	3. 79	2. 63	2. 50	2. 94	3. 10	2. 68	4. 24	4. 59
Culture, sports and entertainment	4. 59	3. 59	3. 18	1. 85	0. 86	1. 13	2. 45	1. 66	1. 60	1. 67	1. 69
Public administration and social organisations	4. 17	4. 81	4. 72	6. 60	4. 91	4. 73	4. 79	3. 99	4. 07	8. 65	9. 57

Source: Department of National Accounts, National Bureau of Statistics. Input-Output Table in China. China Statistics Press, 2012.

Chapter 6.3.5 Analyses of Indicators in "Dematerialisation"

"Dematerialisation" is the reduction of materials at both ends of the production, that is, the reduction of material inputs and pollution emissions. Due to the difference in the development level of the producer service industry, the difference in the service input rate or the material input rate of each city directly leads to the difference in the degree of "dematerialisation". From 2005 to 2010, the energy consumption per unit of the gross domestic product decreased in Beijing, Tianjin, Shanghai and Chongqing. Beijing was the highest which fell by 26.59%, and Shanghai was the lowest which fell by 20.00%. While maintaining the high economic growth rate, the four cities improved the efficiency of economic growth by increasing service input and promoting technological progress, which achieved the "relative dematerialisation". However, due to the "rebound effect", the sharp increase in the consumption of goods has also led to an increase in total material consumption, which was reflected as the increase in the total amount of industrial emissions and solid waste. Chongqing had the largest increase in the total amount of pollutant gases, which increased by 199.40% in 2010, compared to 2005. The largest amount of industrial solid waste was produced in Tianjin, which increased by 65.81% in 2010, compared to 2005. Compared to these cities, the amount of industrial pollutant gases and industrial solid waste increased the least in Beijing, which increased by 34.48% and 2.50% respectively. This is mainly are to Beijing's service economy, especially the development of the producer service industry. The reduction in the total discharge of industrial waste water was mainly caused by the construction and use of urban sewage treatment plants that significantly improved the rate of sewage treatment in urban areas. In order to ultimately achieve "absolute dematerialisation" of the urban economy, it is necessary to increase the income level while increasing the intermediate input of the producer service industry to guide the change of the consumption structure and reduce the rebound effect.

Table 6. 5 Comparison of indicators for "dematerialisation" in Beijing, Tianjin, Shanghai, and Chongqing from 2005 to 2010

Indicators	Year / City	2005	2006	2007	2008	2009	2010	Change (%)
Energy consumption per unit of the gross domestic product (Tons of standard coal/RMB in ten thousand)	Beijing	0. 792	0. 760	0. 714	0. 662	0. 606	0. 582	-26. 59
	Tianjin	1. 046	1. 069	1. 016	0. 947	0. 836	0. 826	-21. 00
	Shanghai	0. 889	0. 873	0. 833	0. 801	0. 727	0. 712	-20. 00
	Chongqing	1. 425	1. 371	1. 333	1. 267	1. 181	1. 127	-20. 95
Total amount of industrial pollutant gases (each 100 million cubic meters)	Beijing	3532	4339	5146	4316	4408	4750	34. 48
	Tianjin	4602	5054	5506	6005	5983	7686	67. 01
	Shanghai	8482	9036	9591	10436	10059	12969	52. 90
	Chongqing	3655	5636	7617	7351	12587	10943	199. 40
Total amount of industrial pollutant water (each 10000 tons)	Beijing	12813	10170	9134	8367	8713	8198	-36. 02
	Tianjin	30081	22978	21444	20433	19441	19680	-34. 58
	Shanghai	51097	48336	47570	41871	41192	36696	-28. 18
	Chongqing	84885	86496	69003	67027	65684	45180	-46. 78
Total amount of industrial solid wastes (each 10000 tons))	Beijing	1238	1356	1275	1157	1242. 4	1269	2. 50
	Tianjin	1123	1292	1399	1479	1515. 7	1862	65. 81
	Shanghai	1964	2063	2165	2347	2254. 6	2448	24. 64
	Chongqing	1777	1764	2087	2311	2551. 8	2837	59. 65

Source: Department of National Accounts, National Bureau of Statistics. China Statistical Yearbook (2011). China Statistics Press, 2012.

Chapter 6.4 The Summary

This book uses the input-output method to conduct a comparative analysis of how developing the producer service industry in Beijing, Tianjin, Shanghai and Chongqing would influence the "dematerialisation" process of urban economy, and draws the following basic conclusions: ① In cities with higher levels of economic development, there would be higher service input rate or lower material input rate. Beijing has begun to transform to the post-industrial era, and the service economy has been relatively developed with the highest service input rate. Shanghai is at the later stage of industrialisation, and the service input rate tended to be more stable. Tianjin and Chongqing are still at the stage of industrialisation with the declining service input rate. ② The proportion of producer services invested to the secondary industry is rising. It shows that China's urban economy is at the stage of industrialisation, and the producer service industry mainly serves the secondary industry. However, the proportion of producer services used in the secondary industry is not high, as the development of the producer service industry is difficult to adapt to the rapid development of the manufacturing industry. On the other hand, it also highlights that the development of the manufacturing industry is more dependent on the input of materials and energy instead of the increase of producer services. ③ At present, urban producer services have little to do with urban economic growth. However, urban economic growth has driven significant demand for producer services. Traditional producer services are mainly promoted in Tianjin and Chongqing, while modern producer services are mainly promoted in Beijing and Shanghai. Therefore, in the sectoral composition of the producer service industry, the proportion of modern producer services, such as financial insurance, technical services and business services, is relatively large in Beijing and Shanghai. The producer service industry in Tianjin and Chongqing is dominated by traditional producer services, such as wholesale and retail, transportation and so on. ④ The differences in the development levels of urban producer services would directly affect the "dematerialisation" process of the urban economy. Although each city has taken certain measures to reduce the energy consumption per unit of the gross domestic product, due to the rebound effect, the total amount of industrial waste gases and solid waste is still relatively large with an upward trend. In cities with relatively developed producer service industry like Beijing and Shanghai, they have relatively small rebound effects while the rebound effect is more significant in Tianjin and Chongqing.

According to the theory of sustainable development, the process of "increasing materialisation" focuses on labor efficiency and ignores ecological efficiency in the quick economic development. At the stage of economic transformation, the adjustment of the economic structure focuses on the ecological efficiency, especially service efficiency. The process of "relative dematerialisation" improves the efficiency of material resources in the production process by the advancement of technology, or reduces production costs and material consumption per unit of products through economies of scale. At the stage of economic maturity, functional changes in the consumption structure focus on ecological efficiency with the a focus on maintaining efficiency, which means that people's consumption patterns begin to change with increase in incomes. In the process of "absolute dematerialisation", economic growth focuses on the improvement of functional services that materials provide to humans, thereby increasing the intermediate input of services in the production process and reducing the dependence on materials. Chongqing is still at the stage of "increasing materialisation", and Tianjin is transforming from the stage of "increasing materialisation" to the stage of "relative dematerialisation". Shanghai is at the stage of "relative dematerialisation", while Beijing is transforming from the stage of "relative dematerialisation" to the stage of "absolute dematerialisation". The main task of sustainable urban economic development is to develop the producer service industry to improve economic growth to achieve "relative dematerialisation". Through improving the economic development level, we would guide the change of the consumption structure and achieve the goal of "absolute dematerialisation".

China is at the middle and later stages of industrialisation and the accelerated development of urbanisation. There are a lot of environmental problems. In particular, the overall deterioration of the environment in large cities has not changed fundamentally. The pressure of "dematerialisation" is gradually increasing. It is necessary to realise the "dematerialisation" of the urban economy by developing the producer service industry. At this stage, the key is to stimulate the demand of the producer service industry and replace the material input with service input. Service industries are also natural, green and "smoke-free". It not only consumes less resources, but also has less environmental pollution with higher added value. It is greatly significant for energy conservation and reduction in consumption. In 2014, the energy consumption per unit of the gross domestic product fell by 4.8%, which had much to do with the development of service industries. The government must change the pattern of economic development in order to achieve "dematerialisation". The government should take the road of new industrialisation and new urbanisation, create conditions for the development of the producer service industry, and promote regional and industrial "dematerialisation". Firstly, preferential policies are introduced to support the development of producer services, especially the development of modern producer services, so as to find new driving force for sustainable economic development. In particular, it is necessary to encourage enterprises to adopt some measures of "dematerialisation", such as outsourcing services and providing services of manufacturing. Like the development of environmentally coordinated products, it transforms from ecological marketing to marketing for sustainable development, and from product-oriented economy to service-oriented economy. Secondly, intensively promoting the transformation of the manufacturing industry increases the demand for producer services and achieves the synchronisation of environmental protection and urban economic development. The government plays a very important role in optimising the economic development by protecting the environment, such as the formulation of new economic indicators for assessment

(green gross domestic product), higher attention paid to the development of service industries for restraint on the low-level urban expansion. The government should eliminate some underdeveloped heavy chemical industries with high energy consumption and low gross domestic product, which is very effective in reducing energy consumption per unit of the gross domestic product. We should strengthen the verification of environmental protection in key industries, encourage enterprises to increase service input rate, actively implement clean production and develop the circular economy for the transformation of economic development pattern. We should impose environmental taxes and approval of emitting pollution to give full play to market mechanisms, so as to promote urban economic transformation. Finally, we should encourage consumer changes in consumer behaviour. According to energy consumption in transportation, the transportation energy consumption of railway and highway buses in China is generally lower than the international average energy consumption. However, China's car market has developed rapidly, which increased by 33% in 2009. At this rate, the number of private vehicles in China would exceed that of the United States and China would within five years become the world's largest gasoline consumer. Therefore, the general public should understand the sustainable lifestyle and participate in activities, such as recycling, green travel and investment, to help the implementation of environmental policies.

Chapter Seven

Policies for Promoting the Development of Urban Producer Service Industry in China

In the process of urban economic transformation, the producer service industry plays a key role in promoting urban industrial transformation and upgrading, optimising the employment structure and proceeding the "dematerialisation", which are reflected in the following aspects. The producer service industry plays an important role in improving industrial labor efficiency and profitability in central cities and megacities. The development of the producer service industry is conducive to the agglomeration of professional talents in the producer service industry to central cities and megacities, and industrial workers are transferred to large cities and medium-sized cities. In the in-depth promotion of urban industrialisation, the role of producer services becomes more and more important in "dematerialisation". Since China is at the stage of industrialisation, the producer service industry mainly helps to improve the level of urban industrialisation. Therefore to study the mechanism of the producer service industry in the development of urban industrialisation, it is important to form an effective urban system based on the division of labor for the needs of industrial agglomeration and integration with the ecosystem, so as to alleviate the pressure of urban resources and the environment and upgrade the position in the value chain as a manufacturer in the value chain.

Chapter 7.1 The Basic Analysis of Urban Industrialisation in China

International experience shows that industrialisation is an inevitable stage in the process of economic development. However, due to the extreme imbalance of regional economic development in China, there are also significant differences in the level of industrialisation in various cities. Therefore, it is necessary to scientifically divide the level of industrialisation of China's cities as a practical basis for giving full play to the role of producer services at different stages of urban industrialisation.

Chapter 7.1.1 The Theoretical Basis for Identification of Stages in Industrialisation

Industrialisation is often defined as the process of increasing the proportion of industry (especially in manufacturing industry) or non-agricultural industries in the gross domestic product, and the process of constantly increasing the proportion of industrial or non-agricultural employees in the total number of employees. However, industrialisation does not only mean an increase in the value of industrial output or employment, but more importantly, an improvement in the quality of industrial development. Therefore, China proposes to promote new industrialisation, emphasising the coordination of economic development with population, resources and the environment, so as to enhance the core competitiveness and capacities of maintaining sustainable development for the urban economy.

Chenery (1969) divided the economic growth process into three stages of pre-industrialisation, industrialisation and postindustrialisation based on the growth of income per capita caused by the transformation of economic structure. The stage of industrialisation was divided into three phases: industry for consumer goods, heavy chemical industry, and high-tech and high value-added industry.[83] In his bookThe Stage of Economic Growth, Rostow divided economic development into six stages according to productivity: the stage of the traditional society, the stage of creating conditions for rapid development, the stage of rapid development, the stage of maturity, the stage of mass and high-value consumption, and the stage of pursuing higher living standards. Hoffmann (1958) believed that the entire process of industrialisation would be the process of increasing the proportion of the industry for capital goods (heavy industry) in the manufacturing industry, that is, the industrialisation. According to the Hoffmann's ratio (the ratio of the industry for consumer goods to the industry for capital goods), industrialisation is divided into four stages of development. At the first stage, the Hoffmann's ratio is about 5, the industry for capital goods is underdeveloped, and the industry for consumer goods dominates the economy. At the second stage, the Hoffman's ratio is about 2.5, and the industry for capital goods is developed, but it is still not as large as the scale of the industry for consumer goods. At the third stage, the Hoffman's ratio is about 1, and the industry for capital goods is roughly equivalent to the industry for consumer goods. At the fourth stage, the Hoffman's ratio is below 1, and the industry for capital goods surpasses the industry for consumer goods and continues to rise.[107] Kuznets (1969) pointed out that the core of changing industrial structure is the "dual transformation" between agriculture and industry. At the early stage of industrialisation, the proportion of agriculture falls below 20%, and the proportion of industry is higher than the proportion of service industries. In the middle of industrialisation, the proportion of agriculture falls below 10%, and the proportion of industry exceeds 50% and becomes the leading industry. At the later stage of industrialisation, the industrial proportion reaches a peak of more than 60%, and service industries begin to develop rapidly. During the period of post-industrialisation, the proportion of service industries would exceed that of industry, accounting for more than 50% and becoming the new leading industry. The greater the proportion of output and employment in service industries, the higher the level of industrial structure.[84] At the early stage of industrialisation, the first to be developed was the logistics industry, such as transportation, wholesale and retail, providing basic producer services for industrialisation. In the middle of industrialisation, there would be the rise of intermediate services, such as financial insurance, architectural design, accounting and legal services. At the later stage of industrialisation, emerging producer services, such as network information, design and development, advertising and exhibitions, would develop rapidly under the promotion of knowledge economy and information technology, and become the main driving force for the improvement of industrialisation. Based on the investment rate and the leading sectors, Rostow (1960) divided the process of industrialisation into six phases: the stage of the traditional society, the stage of creating conditions for rapid development, the stage of rapid development, the stage of maturity, the stage of mass and high-value consumption, and the stage of pursuing higher living standards.[108]

Table 7. 1 Indicators at different stages of industrialisation

Basic indicators	Pre-industrialisation	Industrialisation			Post-industrialisation
		Early stage	Middle period	Later stage	
Gross domestic product per capita US dollars in 2010	750~1500	1500~3000	3000~6000	6000~12000	12000
Structure of output value in three industries	Ⅰ>Ⅱ>Ⅲ	Ⅱ>Ⅰ>Ⅲ	Ⅱ>Ⅲ>Ⅰ	Ⅱ>Ⅲ>Ⅰ	Ⅲ>Ⅱ>Ⅰ
Proportion of output value in industry	Less than 20%	20%~40%	40%~50%	50%~70%	Maintain stable to decline
Degree of non-agricultural labor	Less than 40%	40%~55%	55%~70%	70%~90%	More than 90%
Urbanisation rate of population	30%以下	30%~50%	50%~60%	60%~75%	More than 75%
Leading industry	Agriculture	Light industry	Heavy chemical industry	Process manufacturing industry	High-tech industry Modern service industry

FSource: Institute of Industrial Economics of Chinese Academy of Social Sciences. The Report on China′s Industrialisation (1995-2010). Social Sciences Academic Press (China), 2012.

Since industrialisation is essentially a process of continuous economic development, this book divides the economic growth into three stages of pre-industrialisation, industrialisation and post-industrialisation based on the criteria of Chenery. The stage of industrialisation is divided into the early stage, middle period and later stage. At the early stage of industrialisation, light industry takes the lead in development, and production capacity and production scale are rapidly expanded. During the middle period of industrialisation, industry becomes more heavy-duty and complex, and production becomes more roundabout. At the later stage of industrialisation, overcapacity starts to occur in industrial production, and cities need to transform and upgrade from industrial cities to service-oriented cities. The criteria for the division of industrialisation are usually based on several indicators, such as gross domestic product per capita, ratio of output value in three industries, proportion of non-agricultural labor, urbanisation rate of population and leading industries (see Table 7.1).[109]

Chapter 7.1.2 The Classification of Stages in China's Urban Industrialisation

As an important spatial carrier of economic development, the scale of cities reflects the capacities of promoting economic agglomeration and market potential, and determines the position in the spatial division. Therefore, based on population this book divides 286 prefecture-level cities in China into five levels: central cities, megacities, large cities, medium-sized cities, and small and medium-sized cities (see Table 7.2). Central cities include 10 cities in the eastern region: Beijing, Tianjin, Shanghai, Nanjing, Guangzhou, Wuhan, Chongqing, Chengdu, Xi'an, and Shenyang. In terms of regional distribution, the number of cities in the eastern, central and western regions is similar. However, there are 40 cities with a population of more than 1 million in the eastern region, accounting for 46% of the total, They are far more than 31 cities in the central region and 28 cities in the western region.

Table 7.2 China's urban classification and regional distribution in 2010

Cities	Population	Eastern area	Central area	Western area	Northeast area	Total
Central cities	More than 5 million	5	1	3	1	10
Megacities	From 2 million to 5 million	16	6	5	3	30
Large cities	From 1 million to 2 million	29	24	20	5	78
Medium-sized cities	From 500000 to 1 million	27	37	26	21	111
Small and medium-sized cities	Less than 500000	10	13	30	4	57
Total		87	81	84	34	286

Source: Department of National Accounts, National Bureau of Statistics. China Statistical Yearbook (2011). China Statistics Press, 2012.

According to the classification of industrialisation stages in Table 7.1, there are 40 central cities or megacities with a population of more than 2 million, the gross domestic product per capita exceeds RMB 75000. Only Beijing, Shanghai, Guangzhou, and Shenzhen have the output value of more than 50% in service industries. They are transforming from the later stage of industrialisation to the stage of post-industrialisation, which is located at the top of the most developed city groups in the region of Beijing-Tianjin-Tangshan, Yangtze River Delta and Pearl River Delta. There are 23 cities that enter the later stage of industrialisation with the gross domestic product per capita of more than RMB 40000, including Foshan, Suzhou, Wuxi, Tianjin, Hangzhou, Ningbo, Changzhou, Qingdao, Nanjing, Zibo, Tangshan, Jinan in the eastern area, Changsha, Wuhan, Hefei, Taiyuan, Zhengzhou, Chengdu, Nanchang in the central area, Dalian, Shenyang, Changchun in the northeast area and Urumqi in the west. There are 12 eastern cities and 14 provincial capitals, and most of them are the economic centres of provinces in the eastern, central and northeast areas. There are 13 cities that enter the middle period of industrialisation with the gross domestic product per capita of more than RMB 20000, including Zaozhuang, Shijiazhuang, Putian, Huai'an and Shantou in the eastern area, Xiangfan in the central area, Harbin in the northeast area and Xi'an, Lanzhou, Kunming, Chongqing, Guiyang and Nanning in the western area, which are mainly the provincial capitals of the less developed cities in the central and western regions.

The industrialisation level of central cities in a region determines the stage of industrialisation in that region. In 2010, the industrialisation level in the east and northeast was at the later stage of industrialisation, and the eastern area was about to enter the second half of the later stage. The industrialisation levels in the central and western regions were during the second half and the first half of the middle period respectively. Generally speaking, there is still a big gap in the level of industrialisation in various regions of China. Most of the regions are during the middle period and later stage of industrialisation. The national income per capita exceeds US $ 4000, entering the middle-income stage and facing a turning point of industrialisation.[110]

Table 7. 3 City ranking of employees in various areas of the producer service industry in 2010

(Unit: 10000 people)

Ranking	Transportation, warehousing and postal services		Information transmission, computer services and software		Finance		Leasing and commercial services		Scientific research, technical services and geological exploration	
	Cities	Population	Cities	Population	Cities	Population	Cities	Population	Cities	Population
1	Beijing	51. 00	Beijing	41. 73	Beijing	27. 24	Beijing	77. 81	Beijing	45. 74
2	Shanghai	36. 30	Shanghai	6. 71	Shanghai	23. 63	Shanghai	18. 64	Shanghai	23. 25
3	Guangzhou	22. 57	Hangzhou	6. 49	Shenzhen	10. 86	Shenzhen	12. 42	Xi' an	9. 07
4	Shenzhen	16. 31	Guangzhou	5. 29	Chongqing	9. 75	Guangzhou	9. 93	Hangzhou	8. 52
5	Wuhan	14. 92	Shenzhen	5. 19	Guangzhou	7. 96	Hangzhou	7. 42	Guangzhou	7. 68
6	Chongqing	13. 45	Xi' an	4. 94	Hangzhou	7. 52	Tianjin	6. 95	Chengdu	6. 85
7	Tianjin	12. 50	Chongqing	2. 55	Tianjin	6. 95	Ningbo	5. 24	Tianjin	6. 47
8	Harbin	10. 83	Nanjing	2. 43	Jinan	5. 94	Shenyang	4. 61	Wuhan	5. 74
9	Shenyang	10. 70	Dalian	2. 42	Xi' an	5. 89	Chongqing	4. 30	Shenzhen	5. 43
10	Xi' an	9. 99	Harbin	2. 29	Wuhan	5. 50	Nanjing	3. 97	Chongqing	5. 39

Source: Department of National Accounts, National Bureau of Statistics. China Statistical Yearbook (2011). China Statistics Press, 2012.

According to different industries, the employment of the producer service industry is mainly concentrated in Beijing, Shanghai, Guangzhou and Shenzhen with high levels of economic development and industrialisation. Beijing and Shanghai have gathered most of the professionals in the producer service industry (see Table 7. 3). However, other cities have also made full use of their geographical advantages or factor endowments for certain development opportunities in some areas of the producer service industry. For example, Wuhan and Chongqing take the advantages as central cities in the region to develop transportation, warehousing and postal services. Xi'an and Hangzhou take the advantages of plentiful colleges and high-quality professionals to develop information transmission, computing services and software, scientific research, technical services and geological exploration. The financial industry in Chongqing and Hangzhou, the industry of leasing and commercial services in Hangzhou and Tianjin are also developing rapidly. In large cities and medium-sized cities, industrial development is the mainstay. Producer services are mainly provided by megacities or branches of large-scale urban enterprises in megacities. This is particularly apparent in the industries of financial insurance, transportation and business services.

Chapter 7. 2 The Agglomeration of the Producer Service Industry and Reconstruction of Urban Area

In 2013, the total gross domestic product reached RMB 56. 88 trillion, and the gross domestic product per capita reached RMB

41804. 71. Based on the World Bank ' s standards and comparable prices, China has become the world's second largest economy after the United States, and the income per capita has reached the level of middle-income countries. However, success in the past does not guarantee what would happen in the future. Every country has its own unique opportunities and challenges at a particular stage of economic development. The key to success in the future lies in whether a country can seize the strategic opportunities, adapt to the era of New Normal economy and enhance the consciousness and initiative to accelerate the transformation of economic development. At the early stage of industrialisation, economic growth is usually driven by the manufacturing industry, followed by wave – style consumption. At the later stage of industrialisation, economic growth is driven by service industries, especially Fordism gradually collapsed in large-scale industrial production. Due to the revolution of information technology, Wentelism quietly is to prominence. Personalised and diversified consumption patterns have gradually become mainstream, and the producer service industry plays an important role in supporting the in-depth development of industrialisation or new industrialisation.

Producer service companies usually agglomerate in megacities or central cities, and technological linkages between the producer service industry and the manufacturing industry develop spatial coordination with synergistic innovation effects. Under the market mechanism, the spatial structure of the producer service industry and the manufacturing industry is during the dynamic process of transformation along with the flow of labor force and capital.This dynamic transformation reconstructs the spatial system in urban areas, thus forming a functional urban system for division of labor around megacities. The formation of a functional urban system for division of labor is conducive to improving the core competitiveness of a country in the global value chain.It is also conducive to improving the carrying capacity of urban resources and the environment for the sustainable development of urban economy.

Chapter 7. 2. 1 The Agglomeration, Factors and Development Patterns of the Producer Service Industry

Since the Second World War, the adjustment of the global value chain has reconstructed the international industrial division of labor.The rapid growth of the producer service industry and its spatial agglomeration reflect the global system of production and control based on cities, influencing urban economic development and spatial reorganisation positively. Different from the location theory for the traditional manufacturing industry, the location of the producer service industry not only depends on linear expansion in the inferior for spatial monopoly, but the core city in a networked layout.In New York, London and Tokyo, international cities have been developed at the top of the urban pyramid, which determines the economic competitiveness of a country to a large extent. In China, Beijing, Shanghai, Guangzhou and Shenzhen have become the main cities of the producer service industry. The regions of Beijing-Tianjin-Hebei, Yangtze River Delta and Pearl River Delta have become the main urban areas that producer service companies agglomerate. The network between the three major city groups constitutes the core connection of China's producer service industry. Most of the cities in the Mainland are in the periphery with relatively less connection in the producer service industry (Zhao & Liu, 2012).[111] In the future, with the adjustment of economic structure and the transformation of development pattern, it is necessary to promote the agglomeration and development of the producer service industry in large cities and megacities, and form the industrial structure led by service economy. It is also important to rely on the areas of industrial agglomeration as carriers to promote the effective interaction between the agglomeration of the producer service industry and the transformation of urban functions. It should be pointed out that the coexistence of agglomeration and separate distribution in the producer service industry is caused by the needs of new economic development and the emergence of flexible production methods, and the improvement of infrastructure, such as the popularisation of information technology and the convenience of transportation. Advanced and highly differentiated producer service companies generally agglomerate in central business districts of central cities or central areas. Low-level and standardised producer service companies tend to locate in the suburbs, forming a regional centre for low-level producer services. This develops the spatial pattern that similar industries agglomerate by category for synergistic distribution.

According to factors that promote the agglomeration of the producer service industry, necessary conditions for industrial development include human resources, financial support, popularisation of information technology, openness, infrastructure, institutional environment, city scale and market potential. However, unlike other industries, the producer service industry has characteristics like intangible output and simultaneous consumption. It often requires face-to-face communication between suppliers and buyers, so it is considered to be the most important factor for the agglomeration of the producer service industry. It is also an important reason for the agglomeration of the producer service industry to be different from the general industrial clusters. Through face-to-face communication, it is beneficial for producer service enterprises to obtain auxiliary services from other enterprises and deliver information accurately and effectively to customers at the same time. Since China's market mechanism is still immature, face-to-face communication would help to increase the trust of both parties, thus reducing unnecessary transaction costs and controlling uncertainties of transactions (Gu, 2011).[112] According to the new economic geography, the producer service industry is differentiated by the combination of learning, sharing, matching and other mechanisms of agglomeration that increase returns to scale and external factors, such as limited land and knowledge spillovers, which would be the fundamental driving force of spatial differentiation of the producer service industry. Agglomeration and separate distribution are the main forces of spatial differentiation in the industry, and the producer service industry forms the dynamic spatial structure in regions (Cui & Yang, 2014).[113] In general, the formation of gathering producer service companies includes endogenous factors, such as complementary symbiosis, knowledge spillovers and needs for innovation, as well as exogenous factors, such as external economy, absorption effects and local policies.

There are a lot of factors affecting the agglomeration of the producer service industry, and different development paths determine various patterns of agglomeration. According to the spatial relationship between the producer service industry and the manufacturing industry, the patterns of the producer service industry is divided into functional agglomeration and agglomeration of industrial chain. ① Functional agglomeration is to reduce the barriers between industries through the division of the value chain, technological innovation, and integration within the industry to achieve "core agglomeration". That is to say, while retaining the core business, auxiliary and non-core tasks are outsourced to strengthen industrial services and enhance the core competitiveness of the industry. ② Agglomeration of industrial chain aims to form industrial clusters with a complete value chain, and divides labor through vertical integration according to the degree of industrial linkages. The same kind of enterprises that produce certain products, the upstream and downstream supporting companies and related service enterprises are gathered together in high density (Zhao et al., 2008).[114] According to the driving force of industrial agglomeration in the producer service industry, the patterns are divided into outsourcing services, agglomeration area and foreign-invested promotion. ① The pattern of outsourcing services has adapted to the general trend of global strategic transfer in industries. As a global manufacturing base, China has created huge opportunities for the development of the producer service industry by adopting the pattern of outsourcing services. ② The pattern of agglomeration area is based on the transportation and information network for the concentration of the relevant professional services and supporting facilities for living conditions reasonably and effectively to form functional clusters of producer service companies in the agglomeration area. ③ The pattern of foreign-invested promotion is to attract multinational companies to set up centres for research, development and operation and regional headquarters in China. This can actively introduce new concepts, advanced technologies and management experience of the international producer service industry to improve the level of industrial agglomeration (He, 2009). [115]

Chapter 7.2.2 The Spatial Coordination of the Producer Service Industry and Manufacturing Industry

The reconstruction of the global value chain shows the characteristics of "separate distribution in large regions and agglomeration in small regions" geographically. On the one hand, every part of the value chain is vertically separated into different segments in the world. On the other hand, the separated value segments agglomerate geographically to form urban industrial clusters. Urban industrial clusters are integrated in the global industrial value chain in different ways to become an important carrier of regional economic development, reflecting urban economic competitiveness directly.The theory of global value chain emphasises that industrial clusters in developing cities must participate in the global division of labor and achieve industrial upgrading through the improved position in the value chain. In the global value chain,we need to upgrade different levels from production process to products, to industrial functions, and finally to the value chain(Liu & Xia, 2009).[116] The spatial relationship between the producer service industry and the manufacturing industry also reflects their position in the value chain. An important basis for the producer service industry and the manufacturing industry is the formation of specialised division of labor and the technological correlation effects in the process of value creation. With the further specialised division of labor,more and more sectors in the manufacturing industry have been separated to form a new area of service industries. However, this separation does not weaken the relationship between each other, but further strengthens technical linkages in the division of labor.This can form new network of technological innovation through the promotion of technological innovation and technological linkages between industries for synergetic innovation in the value chain and improvement of the technical level in the entire industry chain.The type of linkage depends on whether the producer service industry is involved in only one aspect or the whole structure to integrate into the basic activities and supporting activities of the manufacturing value chain.It determines that the relationship would be complementary, extended or alternative. Regardless of the type, the highly linked value chain is the premise.

Technological innovation is the internal motivation, and the external conditions include the relaxed supervision and perfect market system. The essence of the integration is the process of continuous construction, deconstruction and reconstruction of the value chain.

The agglomeration of producer service companies has significantly increased the total factor productivity of the local manufacturing industry by knowledge spillovers, flow of the labor force, input sharing, risk pooling and competition. Different from other industries, the producer service industry requires face-to-face communication to increase the trust of both parties and reduce unnecessary transaction costs. Although the communication is so developed nowadays, face-to-face communication is particularly important in the areas of the producer service industry, such as business and finance, which means that the influencing power of the producer service industry has spatial boundaries. The further the geographical distance between the producer service industry and the manufacturing industry, the smaller effects of spillover. Therefore, due to the distance with clients, the producer service industry tends to further develop in cities with the developed manufacturing industry. In this way, the larger the city, the stronger the attraction to the producer service industry. Of course, the perfection of policies directly affects the spillover effects of the producer service industry on the profitability of the manufacturing industry, which helps both sides to form a better relationship of interactive development. Transaction costs also play an important role in spatial coordination, and measures to reduce transaction costs would be beneficial to the coordinated development and upgrading of urban industries (Chen & Chen, 2011).[117] As China's economy is still in the period of transformation, there are significant differences in the level of economic development and the institutional environment. between the eastern and western regions In the eastern region with high level of economic development and marketisation, the interaction between the producer service industry and the manufacturing industry is more prominent, and the development of the producer service industry is more conducive to enhancing the competitiveness of the manufacturing industry.

Although the agglomeration of producer service companies is conducive to supporting the upgrading of spatial layout in the manufacturing industry, the contribution rate varies in different regions. According to comparative advantages, the manufacturing industry has comparative advantages in small cities, and the producer service industry has comparative advantages in large cities. In other words, the scale of cities has important impacts on prioritising the development of different industries and guiding the coordinated positioning of the producer service industry and the manufacturing industry. This determines the difference in the priority of industrial development. Big cities promote the agglomeration and development of the producer service industry first, so as to promote the transformation and upgrading of the manufacturing industry. Small and medium-sized cities must first develop industrial clusters of the manufacturing industry in order to attract clusters of the producer service industry. Since the output efficiency of the producer service industry is higher than that of the manufacturing industry, its high ability to afford the land costs leads to the agglomeration of the producer service industry in central cities and the manufacturing companies can only locate in the outer area. In the cycle of this process, the producer service industry would intensively agglomerate in the centre of large cities (Chen & Chen, 2011).[117] For example, 48 enterprises listed in the Fortune 500 established headquarters in Beijing in 2013, which surpassed Tokyo for the first time and ranked first in the world. The main reason was that Beijing had advantages of information, developed infrastructure, abundant human resources and open policies for investment promotion. Beijing has established eight economic agglomeration areas of headquarters, four economic development zones of headquarters and six industrial clusters of business services. Each economic zone has complete supporting facilities and government services. The economic organisation of multinational corporations is actually at the high end of the industrial chain, which is highly correlated with Beijing's core functions, such as science and technology, information, decision-making power and culture. The agglomeration of producer service companies can lead to an increase in the degree of industrial specialisation. While facing more diversified industries, the knowledge-intensive production and spillover effects would be more obvious, promoting the producer service industry to develop in the area for spatial layout and further agglomerate. The development of the corporate headquarters in a region would generate a large amount of demand for producer services, and further attract producer service companies to locate there. That is to say, the characteristics of agglomeration in the producer service industry have led to the optimal allocation of resources in the eastern regions with good basic conditions, especially in central cities. It also reflects the "Matthew effect" of technical efficiency.

In the open economy, foreign direct investment in the producer service industry also plays an important role in the spatial layout of the manufacturing industry through direct and indirect means. That is, directly improving the production efficiency of manufacturing enterprises by vertical linkages between industries, or indirectly affecting the production efficiency through the local producer service industry and horizontal spillover effects within the industry. Foreign direct investment in the producer service industry can significantly improve the production efficiency of foreign-invested manufacturing enterprises, but it has less effects on the improvement of production efficiency of domestic-funded manufacturing enterprises. The main reason is that foreign direct investment in the producer service industry has an obvious tendency to serve foreign-invested manufacturing companies in order to break barriers in the local market. Therefore, when a city formulates corresponding investment policies for foreign direct investment in the producer service industry, it can indirectly attract foreign direct investment in the producer service industry through the manufacturing industry, especially the advanced manufacturing companies with foreign direct investment. This would not only improve the quality of a country's manufacturing industry, but also improve the overall industrial structure of foreign direct investment. At the same time, it should also be noted that the effects of promoting the development of the high-end manufacturing industry tends to weaken the producer service industry with the increase in the amount of foreign direct investment attracted by the modern producer service industry, although it is useful to the development of the high-end manufacturing industry. Moreover, foreign direct investment in the producer service industry enables foreign-funded institutions to control domestic enterprises and even monopolise certain important industries through technology, branding and market, which would bring certain risks to China's industrial security and affect the sustainable development of urban economy.

Although the synergistic development of the producer service industry and the manufacturing industry is conducive to innovation, the business structure dominated by processing has separated the industrial linkage between the producer service industry and the manufacturing industry, which has affected the effective demand of the manufacturing industry for producer services. The relatively underdeveloped producer service industry is the inevitable result of the export-oriented economic development strategy in China. The development of processing and manufacturing industry competes with the producer service industry in resource allocation, which restricts the development of the producer service industry. Chinese enterprises have been suppressed by the global industrial value chain of multinational corporations, and the demand for producer services has decreased dramatically. This is also the main reason for the long-term, low-level development of China's producer service industry and the reversed trend of "providing services" in the economy. At the same time, the underdevelopment of the producer service industry has led to the lack of high-end input in the manufacturing industry, so the manufacturing industry has been at the low end of the global value chain with high dependence on development path for the long run (Jiang & Liu, 2010).[118] Therefore, transforming export-oriented strategies that focus on processing and manufacturing, reducing the business of processing and manufacturing and introducing the industry for capital goods as a replacement would be vital to construct the national industrial value chain. This is the internal requirement of China to promote the transformation of the producer service industry and realise the transformation of the economic development pattern.

Chapter 7.2.3 The Agglomeration of the Producer Service Industry and Reconstruction in Urban Areas

Due to the development of the concept of "spatial flow", the research of the global urban system has also shifted from the "essence to the network", which becomes the mainstream nowadays. The network between cities determines the status of each city. The global urban system reflects a city's strategic position and rights as a controller. The corresponding level is reflected by the network of its economic and spatial organisation. Producer service companies are the boosters of urban economy and the builders of urban networks. This is also the premise of conducting research on urban network. International cities are the service centres in the global network. Networking between producer service companies is the core of building a global urban system. Through face-to-face communication, the non-material flows of information, ideas, knowledge and education between producer service companies are connected together, so there is a strong correlation between the networks of transportation and business (Zhao & Chen, 2011).[111] The agglomeration of the producer service industry mainly promotes urban transformation through industrial transfer, spatial reorganisation, allocation of resources, transfer of factors and structural adjustment. The driving force of urbanisation and urban expansion comes from the industrial promotion led by the producer service industry. The essence of urban industrial transformation and systematic reconstruction is the improvement of urban functions and the optimisation of spatial layout driven by industrial upgrading. With the improvement of the level of economic development, the producer service industry would certainly replace the manufacturing industry as the fundamental driving force for urban transformation and development and the ability to enhance the sustainable development of the economy.

According to spatial layout and value chain in urban areas, there is a mechanism of forming industrial agglomeration in the manufacturing industry and the producer service industry with the dual effects of agglomeration. The scale of cities is conducive to the improvement of dual effects of agglomeration. The central city of a city group has certain influence over the dual effects of agglomeration in other cities. The shorter the distance, the greater the influences, and the dual effects of agglomeration has an "inverted U-shaped" effect on labor productivity (Li, 2013).[119] Returns to scale become more and more obvious in the agglomeration of the producer service industry, which occur in national and provincial central cities. Producer service companies agglomerate intensively in central cities, such as Beijing, Shanghai, Guangzhou and Shenzhen. The producer service industry and the manufacturing industry clearly show a regional integration that the producer service industry agglomerates in central area and the manufacturing industry produces goods in the inferior (Wang et al., 2014).[120] The producer service industry and the manufacturing industry have different mechanisms of spatial distribution. Producer service companies mainly agglomerate in regional central cities, while manufacturing companies mainly agglomerate around the central cities of coastal areas. Both of them have an "crowding out effect" within a city. While Beijing's producer services are constantly strengthening, the manufacturing functions are gradually moved to other areas. The "central effect" is reflected by the role of Shanghai's producer service industry in promoting the city and the surrounding manufacturing companies. As a result, the Yangtze River Delta has formed a spatial pattern with a centre for the producer service industry in Shanghai and manufacturing bases in Jiangsu and Zhejiang. The producer service industry in Shanghai not only promotes the development of local manufacturing industry, but also positively influences the two major manufacturing bases in Jiangsu and Zhejiang, which boosts the regional economy. However, in addition to mutual promotion, the producer service industry in Shanghai and the surrounding cities would show an industrial pattern of competition and complementarity. Shanghai has gathered more high-end producer services, while secondary cities and small and medium-sized cities have gathered low-end producer services. The degree of differentiation in the producer service industry is basically consistent with city rankings.

However, the integration of urbanisation and the producer service industry in China is generally poor, and it is still in the break-in period. The agglomeration and development of the producer service industry cannot meet the needs of reconstructing the urban system. In the process of deepening the new urbanisation and industrialisation, we should strengthen the strategic understanding of the integration and development of urbanisation and the producer service industry. While formulating policies of the urbanised supporting facilities for the producer service industry, we should pay attention to the underdevelopment of the producer service industry and the improvement of urbanisation. There would be some doubts in the development of the producer service industry. In the context of deepening international division of labor, the producer service industry is at the high end of the value chain, it is an important reason for bringing high value-added to developed countries. However, excessively developing the scale of the producer service industry would lead to the disconnection between the virtual economy and the real economy in these developed countries. When facing the impacts of the global economic crisis, it would accelerate the economic recession, requiring a long period to recover (Xu & Liu, 2014).[121] Under the current national conditions, the opportunity cost of investing a large amount of capital into producer service enterprises is greater than that in manufacturing enterprises, and the financial and economic benefits are not as good as that of the manufacturing industry. Therefore, we need further analyse "developing service industries as an important way to upgrade the industrial structure and transform the economic growth pattern". At present, the focus of development must further promote the international competitiveness of China's manufacturing industry, so as to make full use of China's high-end demographic dividend, which would lead to the rapid growth of China's economy (Li, 2013).[122]

Although there are different views on promoting the development of the producer service industry, it is undeniable that the agglomeration of producer service companies plays a key role in promoting the optimisation of urban spatialsystem. At present, the agglomeration of China's producer service industry is still relatively lagging behind. The possible policies mainly include the following aspects. ① We should focus on the producer service industry, in terms of development strategies. It is vital to break the cycle of "low-end manufacturing, low-end producer services". In the process of upgrading the manufacturing industry, we should be able to provide high-end industrial producer services and actively develop advanced manufacturing industries. We need to increase the demand for producer services by taking advantage of the highly roundabout production process for the development trend of providing services for national economy and manufacturing. It is also important to increase investment in the producer service industry, scientifically develop the producer service industry and increase the supply of technology-intensive and knowledge-intensive producer services(Jiang & Li,2013).[123] ② We should change strategitic focus from on processing to general business.The development of processing business under the global value chain division has shifted the production factors to the manufacturing industry and has a "crowding out effect" on the producer service industry.In the long run,processing business has a low rate of procurement,a short value chain,and low degree of localising components in China. Normally, only a few local companies can participate in the supply side. The entire production chain of general trade is carried out in China, forming a complete domestic industrial chain. The manufacturing industry has a large intermediate demand for producer services, so it can drive the development of the producer service industry. As China's economic strength increases,the intermediate demand of general trade for services continues to increase. Therefore, industrial linkages and spatial coordination can be functioning fully, which is conducive to the development of the producer service industry. ③ We should improve core competitiveness and respond to economic globalisation. The producer service industry has changed the original structure and level in the division of labor by the roundabout production of the manufacturing industry and the extension of the industrial chain.It can also directly contribute to the horizontal extension of the global value chain into two different industrial value chains for manufacturing and services.While facing to the "waterfall effect" and "pressure of saving resources" in the global service chain, China must recognise the complexity of current competition in the producer service industry and actively respond to the severe challenges from multinational companies. Therefore, China needs to intensively develop the producer service industry, seek coordinated and mutual development of the manufacturing industry and service industries, realise the steady growth of the economy, and solve the imbalance of industrial structure in economic development by the cross externalities of both sides, so as to promote China to the high end of the global value chain (Huang, 2013).[124]

Chapter 7.3 Policies for Promoting the Development of Urban Producer Service Industry

Under the profound changes of the global division of labor and the increasing restraints on resources and environment, cities are facing unprecedented opportunities and challenges. The experience of developing international cities shows that we can promote urban industrial upgrading, improve urban economic functions and urban innovation capabilities by creating conditions to form clusters of producer service companies and developing the producer service industry, so as to hold a favourable position in the division of labor for the global value chain and enhance the core competitiveness of the urban economy. In the future, China's urbanisation would "transform" from rapid expansion to quality improvement. It is necessary to rely on large cities and focus on small and medium-sized cities to gradually form city groups with great influencing power and promote the coordinated development of large, medium-sized and small cities and small towns for new urbanisation which is intensive, functional, green and low-carbon. Therefore, in the process of industrialisation and market-oriented reforms, China should grasp the development trend of industrial clusters and integration with the focus on the ecosystem to create the external conditions for the development of the producer service industry and the sustainable urban economic development.

Chapter 7. 3. 1 Optimising Technological Paths of Industrialisation and Transforming Economic Developm-ent Patterns

The core of transforming the economic development pattern is the optimisation of technological routes for industrialisation and the transformation of operational systems (Jin, 2011).[125] At the early stage of China's industrialisation, we rely mainly on the input of traditional production factors, and the scale of industrial production has been rapidly expanded under the lower technological development level. However, this development pattern with low added value and high pollution is facing increasing pressure from resources and the environment. With the development of industrialisation, the rising prices of production factors, such as land and labor, have gradually lost the original comparative advantages in cities. To realise the transformation of technological routes for industrialisation, the key is that industrial development should rely more on technological innovation and improvement of labor quality, reducing dependence on resources for less environmental damage. As a sector of outputting knowledge and technology, the producer service industry determines its expansion of scale and performance by the capabilities of making innovations, which directly affects the core competitiveness of industries in cities. In 2010, China had the largest number of scientific and technological human resources, research and development personnel in the world. The number of international scientific papers ranked second in the world, and the number of patented inventions created by Chinese people ranked third globally. China had the fourth largest number of applications to "the Patent Cooperation Treaty" in the world, and the funds for research and development ranked third globally. All of these set up the foundation for the development of advanced producer service industry and optimisation of technological routes for industrialisation. Therefore, cities must rely on the producer service industry to establish a system of core technological innovations for high-end manufacturing to achieve a shift in strategic transformation to high value-added industries and economic development.

The urban economic development should take the producer service industry as the strategic focus of economic reorganisation. The main task is to promote the effective interaction between new industrialisation and urbanisation, and to transform the focus from material resources to knowledge and technology. Firstly, the National Comprehensive Reform Experimental Zone for Producer Services would be built in central cities like Beijing and Shanghai. In particular, it is necessary to encourage large-scale and high-quality producer service enterprises with good reputation to implement cross-regional and cross-industry mergers and acquisitions in accordance with market mechanisms, and become clusters of producer service companies with special features, such as financial services in Hailujiazui, Shanghai, and information services in Zhongguancun, Beijing. We should encourage them to become bigger and more competitive, thus serving the industrialisation level of the entire urban system. Secondly, the government must rationally guide the investment, strengthen the construction of infrastructure projects highly relating to the producer service industry and scientifically plan all kinds of infrastructure to form a system of division of labor with reasonable functions and outstanding comparative advantages. We should formulate a set of policies to promote the development of producer services, including policies of fiscal aspects, financing, land, talents and incentives. The government should give tax incentives and relieve the restricition for reviewing loans to reduce financing costs, and enjoy equal benefits in the use of resources. For example, we can use debt financing and equity financing to effectively expand investment and financing channels for producer service enterprises. It is also vital to charge materials, like water, electricity, gas and land in the production, as the same price in industries, and encourage the training, development and introduction of talents in the producer service industry. Especially in the case of relatively difficult economic situation in developed countries, we should launch policies to introduce international professional talents for strategic reserve of high-end talents in the producer service industry, so as to build a base of talents for the development of industrial strategic centres. Finally, the focus of government policies on optimising technological routes for industrialisation cannot be limited to the scale and output in enterprises. We should improve the output capacity of innovation, especially the output capacity of independent innovation focusing on "brand, patent, technical standards, and technological advancement". In particular, the establishment of a technological innovation platform in the agglomeration area of the producer service industry would develop a technological innovation network with strong innovation capabilities. In Beijing, Shanghai, Xi'an, Wuhan, Chongqing and other cities with many universities and research institutions, the government should support the integration of industry, academia and research to give full play to local human resources and scientific and technological research and development, and encourage the development of intermediary service institutions in science and technology innovation and emerging producer services.

Chapter 7.3.2 Promoting the Reform of a Market-Oriented System and Innovating a Pattern of Outsourcing Services

An important reason for the underdevelopment of China's producer service industry is that the low degree of industrialisation and marketisation restricts the increase in demand for producer services. Due to the direct or indirect monopoly of state-owned enterprises in some areas of the producer service industry, such as banking, insurance, telecommunications, postal services, civil aviation, railway, shipping, the entry barriers are increased to limit the basic role of the market in the allocation of resources in the producer service industry. In this way, the industry lacks competition, and it is difficult to improve the degree of specialisation to cope with the fierce competition of foreign-funded enterprises. It would also increase the cost of producer services, reduce the demand for outsourcing business of producer services, and affect the expansion of the market scale, leading to the inefficiency of economic operation in cities. At the same time, as the producer service industry is contract-intensive, it is difficult to make forward-looking institutional innovations in the process of transformation in China's cities. The high degree of market intervention often results in the over agglomeration of office buildings in the promotion of constructing central business districts in urban areas. The long-term economy of "administrative districts" caused by market segmentation and household registration has restricted urban expansion and the free flow of labor for the long term, resulting in the serious insufficiency of professional talents for the development of the producer service industry and limiting the scale economy of cities and the specialisation of the urban system.

Therefore, promoting the system reform of service enterprises and optimising the market environment are the primary measures to promote the development of China's urban producer service industry. Firstly, central cities and megacities should accelerate the institutional reform of state-owned enterprises in the producer service industry, improve business management, innovate patterns to provide services, strengthen the corporate competitiveness and capabilities of serving the regional industrial development. In the economic globalisation, the producer service industry would gradually open to foreign investment, and those measures can cope with the intensified market competition and threats caused by direct foreign investment in the development of China's producer service enterprises. At the same time, large and medium-sized cities with relatively incomplete market systems should reduce unnecessary industrial controls, reduce barriers to market entry, and encourage and guide private companies into the producer service industry. We need to treat private companies fairly in the market, strengthen the mechanism in competition, including comprehensive industrial standards, regulation of behaviour in the market and proper guidance on the new business of producer services. This can gradually break up the unreasonable monopoly in industries in the producer service industry. Secondly, the government should improve the relevant laws and regulations of the producer service industry. We need to establish an open, transparent, efficient and standardised system of market supervision to regulate behaviour, eliminate institutional barriers, reduce the risk of cooperation in outsourcing business of services and transaction costs, so as to implement strategies of outsourcing services for industrial companies. Although the conditions of perfect infrastructure, developed information technology and advanced business buildings are important, corporations prefer cities with regulated market operations, perfect trading systems, transparent implementation of policies, efficient government and effective legal protection.

With the development of communication and information technology, the proportion of trade in services has increased significantly in the international trade, accounting for more than 20%, while the proportion was only 12.5% in China. In order to make full use of the high-quality resources of countries around the world, improve the life cycle of new products, and reduce risks of product development, developed countries have integrated the global value chain through outsourcing services to reduce the production and operating costs of enterprises, so as to focus on the strategic part of the value chain, research and development of high-end technology and products. It can promote the transformation and upgrading of urban industries, which allows the international cities to maintain at the top of the international division of labor in the urban system. Due to the large number of manufacturing orders from developed countries, the principle is to develop supporting services, such as finance, accounting, law, business, consulting and advertising, in order to control profits of core industries, guarantee the quality of services, and maintain the competitiveness of enterprises. For developing countries, outsourcing services can change the principle that service industries can only develop rapidly at the stage of post-industrialisation for the upgrading of industrial structure. Of course, multinational corporations have begun to organise scientific research institutions around the world, promoting the exchanges and cooperation between countries in high-tech fields. In particular, they have outsourced offshore services with certain development standards and processes, such as information technology services, industrial design, and software development, to developing countries, such as China and India, which promoted the development of local producer service companies. However, China's enterprises for outsourcing services are still at the primary stage for growth, the management is relatively backward, the investment and financing channels are limited, and the funds are seriously scarce. The lack of supporting funds has seriously affected the development of the entire industry.

In order to grasp opportunities in the new round of transferring the producer service industry, China's central cities and megacities should base on the heterogeneity of the producer service industry and the differences in urban development to make full use of their late-mover advantages and actively expand the areas of Information Technology Outsourcing (ITO) and Business Process Outsourcing (BPO). This can improve the automation of the production process and the engagement of information technology in production and management, and create conditions for significant economic development. The first is to attract high-tech multinational companies, such as Microsoft and SAP, to establish regional headquarters or institutions of research and development in China's developed central cities or large cities. By introducing advanced patterns to develop products and manage enterprises, we can provide high-end and professional services to drive the improvement of service quality in the industry and the expansion of the total. Under the premise of ensuring national economic security, we need to actively guide domestic and foreign venture capital flows to enterprises in outsourcing business of services, encourage local producer service companies and multinational companies to cooperate and establish strategic alliances. It is also important to benefit from knowledge spillovers, demonstration of management and scale of cooperation to improve the international competitiveness of China's producer service enterprises. The second is to improve the protection of intellectual property rights. Due to the lack of attention to intellectual property rights in the past, there were a lot of pirate products in the domestic market. It is common to plagiarise creativity in the producer service industry, which would restrict the capabilities of making innovations in the market through the mechanism of "eliminating the good by the bad". Therefore, setting up special institutions for intellectual property rights in developed central cities or large cities not only protects the interests of foreign producer service enterprises in China, but also helps China's producer service industry to learn from advanced enterprises under market regulation. This can improve the level of China's producer service industry through introduction, learning, analysis and re-innovation.

Chapter 7. 3. 3 Promoting the Layout in Industrial Clusters and Improving Urban Division of Labor

The underdevelopment of urbanisation and the separation of industrial layout in China have weakened the demand for the producer service industry, resulting in the lack of necessary conditions to develop the producer service industry and support the industrial chain effectively. Producer services that could have been provided through outsourcing have to be completed within industrial enterprises, because the degree of specialisation is too weak or the price is too expensive. Clusters are the important carriers for the agglomeration and development of the producer service industry with external economies like economies of scale, reduction in costs, and innovation. More producer service companies with synergy and learning effects agglomerate in certain areas. The upcoming economies of scale and efficient innovation would be inevitable in the development of the spatial structure of service industries. In China, most of cities are industrial cities, and the manufacturing industry is the mainstay of the national economy. China's industrialisation rate is 40%, making it the largest manufacturing country in the world. The development of the manufacturing industry would lead to the demand for producer services, which is the premise for the development of the producer service industry. As the manufacturing industry becomes increasingly high-end in agglomeration, more and more producer services are not supplied within the manufacturing industry but outsourced in the market. A large number of professional areas in the producer service industry have begun to emerge and attract more and more investment. Therefore, central cities and megacities with good conditionsin China have begun to develop clusters in the producer service industry as the main way to improve the sustainable development of urban economy. Due to the increased restraints on resources and the environment, clusters of the producer service industry can increase the degree of industrial agglomeration, which is conducive to energy conservation, efficient use of land, and improved economic operational efficiency.

Therefore, it is necessary to develop the producer service industry as an industrial bond to build the urban structure scientifically and rationally. Large, medium-sized and small cities, small towns and city groups should be scientifically arranged and closely linked with regional economic development and industrial layout for the carrying capacity of resources and the environment. Firstly, it is necessary to promote the formation of industrial structure based on producer services in central cities and megacities and develop clusters of the producer service industry. With certain development levels in cities, economic structural changes and environmental constraints, the pattern of agglomeration in the producer service industry would change from a single large central business district to several smaller specialised central business districts with multi-polarisation and decentralisation, namely the classified clusters of the producer service industry. London, New York, and Tokyo and other world-class cities have all experienced the formation of network from a single central business district to several smaller specialised central business districts, so as to form the network of service institutions and solve excessive concentration of business functions and high operating costs in central areas. At present, only Beijing and Shanghai have relatively mature central business districts, while the central business districts are still under construction in

Guangzhou and Shenzhen. In central cities with good basic conditions and large regional economic scale, it is necessary to give full play to the role of market mechanisms and promote the development of urban central business districts. We should attract large enterprises to locate in clusters of the producer service industry, transfer the manufacturing base to the neighbouring cities with comparative advantages, and realise the optimal spatial combination between the corporate value chain and regional resources. This can also form clusters of the producer service industry with important impacts on the regional economic development, providing important support for the industrialisation of the region. The second is to setop industrial transfer policies, promote the separation of the producer service industry and industry, and encourage industrial enterprises to move to the surrounding area of large cities or other cities. This can create conditions for the relocation and agglomeration of the producer service industry and industrial enterprises to achieve the rational allocation of labor resources and structural optimisation in industrial transfer. In the past, the industrial layout of China's cities was characterised by planned economy and "administrative districts". The market mechanism did not function fully, which seriously restricted the development of specialised division of labor. Only by giving full play to the fundamental role of market mechanisms in allocating resources, can we transfer the industry rationally and form reasonable industrial clusters. Central cities and megacities cities can influence the surrounding area through the producer service industry. Large cities would become new industrial centres and manufacturing bases, while small and medium-sized cities by usy the vertical division of industries and the derivation of the industrial chain benefit from the influencine of large-scale industries, so as to form the development pattern of integration, division of labor, and complementary advantages among cities. Clusters of the producer service industry in central cities or megacities integrate different areas, such as financial insurance, logistics, research, development and design, advertising, and exhibitions. With the support of policies, there would be strategic development of the producer service industry in a relatively short period of time as a regional economic centre. This can provide necessary producer services for the transformation and upgrading of the manufacturing base in the regional economy, allowing industrial enterprises to focus on strategic activities and improve the level of the industrialisation and integration of the industrial chain.

Chapter 7. 3. 4 Accelerating the Development of Industrial Integration and Improving Ability to Innovate Independently

The producer service industry has the characteristics of intermediate investment in a close relationship with the primary and secondary industries and the service industry for living standards. It is the product of division of labor and externalisation of services. The producer service industry mainly provides intermediate services for other industries. At the stage of industrialisation, it mainly serves the advancement of industrialisation. Although China ' s industry has achievedrapid development after the reform and opening up, it is still at the stage of extensive development, which takes mainly advantages of resource input and labor cost, forms low-level and fierce competition in the manufacturing process and stays at the low end of the value chain. With increased costs of factors, especially the deterioration of the external economic environment, it is difficult to develop China's manufacturing industry. Therefore, enterprises prefer "internalisation of producer services" and form an organisational structure of "large and complete" or "small but complete" in order to resolve the risks of management as much as possible and generate effective demand for producer services. The shrinking market in the producer service industry has limited the specialised division of labor and restricted the effective support for the manufacturing industry. In this vicious circle, foreign-funded enterprises are in a leading position in many advanced areas of the producer service industry, like accounting and auditing, industrial design, research and development. In this case, foreign-funded enterprises use the strategy of "re-focusing" to further strengthen their competitive advantages. However, China's industrial enterprises have to support foreign-funded enterprises and cannot rise in the value chain.

The producer service industry is the result of the industry, and its development is largely based on the demand from other industries, especially the needs for industrialisation. In order to accelerate the development of the producer service industry, we must grasp the opportunities of industrial integration, strengthen the division of labor in the industry chain, continuously the interaction and linkages between industries. Firstly, we should accelerate to develop outsourcing business of services and strengthen the professional division of labor. The government can guide and promote industrial enterprises to carry out management innovation and reconstruction of business processes through financial subsidies and credit guarantees. This can transform some non-core producer services into externalised professional services, and integrate enterprises' capabilities of supplying services with core competitive advantages for specialised management and the increasingly specialised division of labor in the industrial chain. The second is to accelerate the development of information technology services. Information technology should be used in the entire production process of enterprises for the enhancement of exchanges and cooperation between departments. Between enterprises, it is very important to promote cooperation between upstream and downstream enterprises through the establishment of information sharing platform. The application of information technology can strengthen the business communication between producer service enterprises and clients, break through the geographical restrictions on the development of the producer service industry and improve the industrial integration of central cities and surrounding cities with the use of high-speed highways and railways to form an effective industrial system for division of labor. The third is to introduce the producer service industry into the production process of the three industries, and strive to increase the added value of products. Producer services are needed in design, development, market research, logistics and transportation, marketing planning to enhance industrial competitiveness, give full play to the industrial correlation effect of the producer service industry, and achieve regional economic integration through industrial division of labor within closely associated city groups to accelerate industrial upgrading. The fourth is to encourage manufacturing companies to focus on core business or "providing services of manufacturing enterprises", benefit from specialisation and take producer services as the important way to improve the competitiveness of enterprises and create profits. This can form new sources for business growth and accelerate the process of "providing services of manufacturing" and "service-oriented manufacturing". The fifth is to develop strategic emerging industries, in the producer service industry such as "energy conservation and environmental protection, information technology, biology, high-end equipment manufacturing, new energy, new materials and new energy vehicles". Through the growth of strategic emerging industries, we would improve the ability of local enterprises to provide professional producer services, such as scientific research, business services, financial services and information services, so as to promote the China's producer service industry to be specialised, high-end, large-scale and international.

Chapter 7.3.5 Regulating the Ecological System for Environmental Pressure

At the early stage of industrialisation, cities are the centre for the manufacturing industry, relying on a large amount of resources to promote economic development. However, the increase in material inputs usually increases pollution and worsens the environment in cities. The traditional pattern of industrialisation often develops the industry first and then deals with the pollution. It is very difficult to govern, some industrial enterprises have to be "shut down, merged and restructured" resulting in the slowdown of economic growth. Therefore, in the process of urban development in China, in order to guarantee the speed and scale of economic growth, the environment was sacrificed. As the level of economic development increases, a number of heavy chemical companies in some central cities and megacities have been transferred, but this administrative measure has only eased the ecological pressure of some cities. They just transfer or move away from the source of pollution, and pollution occurs in other cities or even a broader area. Overall, it increases the burden on resources and the environment, but does not solve the pollution fundamentally. The increase in the input of producer services in the industrial production chain can reduce the dependence of industry on energy consumption and resource input, and promote the role of knowledge and technology in the process of industrialisation, which is conductive to the ecological and high-end development of industry.

Based on the industrial ecosystem, we should make rational industrial regulations to guide industrial enterprises to expand outsourcing business of services, stimulate the demand of producer services, and increase "green" employment while reducing "brown" employment. Firstly, according to the "3R principle (reduce, reuse, recycle)", we need to formulate new indicators for economic assessment (green gross domestic product), attach importance to the development of the producer service industry, and constrain the low-level expansion of urban areas. The government should eliminate some underdeveloped heavy chemical industries with high energy consumption and low gross domestic product, which is very effective in reducing energy consumption per unit of the gross domestic product. We should strengthen the verification of environmental protection in key industries, encourage enterprises to increase service input rate, actively implement clean production and develop the circular economy for the transformation of economic development pattern. We should impose environmental taxes and approval of emitting pollution to give full play to market mechanisms, so as to find new sources for sustainable economic development. Clean production would involve more follow-up activities of producer services, such as inspections and maintenance, reducing the investment in energy and materials while increasing the input of labor input, that is, the increase in employment. At the same time, clean production would also encourage companies to install automated processing equipment, increasing the automation of production. The second is to promote the division and policies of the industrial value chain through environmental rules and policies, stimulate the development of the producer service industry in a broader field, so as to increase the capacities of absorbing the labor force and promote the orderly flow of labor. The problem that "expenditure is controlled by pollution" is caused by environmental regulations, and it would increase the production costs of industrial enterprises in urban areas to reduce the scale of production or move to cities with larger ecological capacities. This can help companies to transfer and upgrade for environmental protection so that industries can be optimally deployed in the urban system. At the same time, industrial enterprises with heavy emission of pollutants can also consider environmental regulations as a competitive factor. The producer service industry can help industrial enterprises to obtain comparative advantages, reduce dependence on resources and bring employment growth. This can effectively avoid the increase of production costs by environmental regulations and, thereby reducing the demand elasticity of products. Therefore, developing the producer service industry can help "double dividends" of energy conservation, reduction in emitting pollutants and employment growth through environmental regulations.

References

[1] Daily, G. Nature Service: Societal Dependence on Natural Ecosystem[M].Washington,D.C: Island Press,1997,75-79

[2] Nijkamp Petal.Sustainable Cities in European [M].London: Earthscan Publications Limited,1994,40-41

[3] Walter Siembab and Bob Walter Betal. Sustainable Cities: Concepts and Strategies for Eco-city Development [M].London: Eco-Home Media,1992,35-37

[4]路易斯·芒福德.城市文化[M].北京:中国建筑工业出版社,2009,10-15

[5] Tjallingii S. P. Ecopolis: Strategies for Eco-logically Sound Urban Development [M].London:Backhuys Publishers,1995,20-22

[6] Yanitsky O.Social Problem of Man's Environment [J].The city and Ecology,1987(1): 174-192

[7] Rigister R.Eco-city Berkeley: Building Cities for A Heathy Future [M].Berkeley,CA: North Atlantic Books,1987,110-115

[8]蒋敏元,陈继红.城市化与城市的可持续发展[J].东北林业大学学报,2003,(3):53-58

[9] Guy S, Henneberry J, Rowley S. Development Cultures and

Urban Regeneration [J].Urban Studies,2002,39(7): 1181-1196

[10]Bugliarello G.Urban Sustainability:Science,Technology and Policies [J].Journal of Urban Technology,2004,(11): 1-11

[11]Machlup F.The Production and Distribution of Knowledge in the United States [M].New Jersey: Princeton University Press,1962, 44-46

[12] Browing & Singelman.The Emergence of a Service Society [M].New York: Springfield,1975,33-37

[13]Greenfield,H.Maupower and the Growth of Producer Services [M].New York:Columbia University Press,1966,53-58

[14] Hansen N. The Strategic Role of Producer Services in Regional Development [J]. International Regional Science Review, 1994,(1-2):976-988

[15] Martinelli F A. The Changing Geography of Advanced Producer Services [M].London:Belhaven Press,1991,77-79

[16]李金勇.上海生产性服务业发展研究[D].[复旦大学博士学位论文].上海:复旦大学,2005,12-14

[17]格鲁伯,沃克.服务业的增长:原因和影响[M].上海:上海三联书店,1993,33-38

[18]冯泰文.生产性服务业的发展对制造业效率的影响——以交易成本和制造成本为中介变量[J].数量经济技术经济研究,2009,(3):56-65

[19]江静,刘志彪,于明超.生产者服务业发展与制造业效率提升:基于地区和行业面板数据的经验分析[J].世界经济,2007,(8):52-62

[20]汪德华,张再金,白重恩.政府规模、法治水平与服务业发展[J].经济研究,2007,(6):51-64

[21]顾乃华.生产性服务业对工业获利能力的影响和渠道——基于城市面板数据和SFA模型的实证分析[J].中国工业经济,2010,(5):48-58

[22]Porter M.Clusters and the New Economics of Competition [J].Harvard Business Review,1998,76(6):77-90

[23]刘明宇,芮明杰,姚凯.生产性服务价值嵌入与制造业升级的协同演进关系研究[J].中国工业经济,2010,(8):66-75

[24]顾乃华,夏杰长.服务业发展与城市转型:基于广东实践的分类研究[J].广东社会科学,2011,(4):67-72

[25]Aguilera A.Services Relationship,Market Area and the Intra-metropolitan Location of Business Services [J].The Service Industries Journal,2003,23(1): 43-58

[26]Coffey W J.Shearmur R G.Agglomeration and Dispersion of High-order Service Employment in the Montreal Metropolitan Region: 1981-1996 [J].Urban Studies,2002,39(3): 360-377

[27]Pandit N R,Cook G.The Benefits of industrial Clustering: Insight from the British Financial Services Industry at three locations [J].Journal of Financial Services Marketing,2003,7(3): 230-245

[28] Daniels P. W. Producer Services Research in the United Kingdom [J].Professional Geographer,1995,5(1):884-906

[29] Harrington J. W. Empirical Research on Producer Service Growth and Regional Development: International Comparisons [J]. Professional Geographer,1995,(1):663-681

[30] Selya R.M.Taiwan as a Service Economy [J].Geoforum, 1994,25(3): 305-322

[31] Francois,J.Trade in Producer Services and Returns Due to Specialization under Monopolistic Competition [J].Canadian Journal of Economics,1990,(23): 199-229

[32] Guerrieri P.and Meliciani V.International Competitiveness in Producer Services[R].Paper Presented at the SETI Meeting Rome, 2003,115-119

[33] Mukesh E.and Ashok K.Agriculture,Innovational Ability, and Dynamic Comparative Advantage of LDCS [J]. Journal of International Trade and Economic Development,2001,10(3):77-89

[34]刘志彪.发展现代生产者服务业与调整优化制造业结构[J].南京大学学报(哲学.人文科学.社会科学),2006,(5):36-44

[35] Coffey W. J. Service Industries in Regional Development [M].Montreal: Institute for Research on Public Policy,1990,46-49

[36] Thompson E.C.Producer Services [R].Kentucky Annual Economic Report,2004,18-23

[37]钟韵,闫小培.建国以来广州生产性服务业成长特征研究[J].热带地理,2007,(4):348-353

[38]陶纪明.上海生产者服务业的空间集聚[M].上海:上海人民出版社,2009,15

[39]赵群毅,谢从朴,王茂军,薛金鑫,刘芳君,李凌.北京都市区生产者服务业地域结构[J].地理研究,2009,(9):1401-1013

[40] Stein R. Producer Services, Transaction Activities, and Cities: Rethinking Occupational Categories in Economic Geography

[J].European Planning Studies,2002,4(6):25-49

[41]赵毅群,周一星.西方生产者服务业空间结构研究及其启示[J].城市规划学刊,2007,(1):19-24

[42]李迅,刘琰.低碳、生态、绿色——中国城市转型的发展战略[J].城市规划学刊,2011,(2):1-7

[43]吴海瑾,李程骅.现代服务业:城市转型的新动力系统[J].现代城市研究,2010,(11):23-28

[44]徐巨洲.探索城市发展与经济长波的关系[J].城市规划,1997,(5):54-58

[45]熊彼特.经济发展理论:对利润、资本、信贷和经济周期的研究[M].北京:中国社会科学出版社,2009

[46]汪光焘.中国城市报告2012/2013[M].北京:外文出版社,2012,25-29

[47]Northam,R.M.Urban Geography [M].New York:John Wiley & Ss,1979,75-79

[48]马歇尔.经济学原理[M].北京:商务印书馆,2005,112-115

[49]Yang,X and Rice,R.An Equilibrium Model Indigenizing the Emergence of a Dual Structure Between the Urban and Rural Sectors [J].Journal of Urban Economics,1994,(25):346-368

[50] Oliva, R. and Kallenberg, R. Managing the Transition from Products to Services [J]. International Journal of Service Industry Management,2003,14(2): 160-172

[51]彼得·霍尔,考蒂·佩因.从大都市到多中心都市[J].国际城市规划,2009,(增刊):319-331

[52]吕政,刘勇,王钦.中国生产性服务业发展的战略选择——基于产业互动的研究视角[J].中国工业经济,2006,(8):5-12

[53]顾乃华.城市化与服务业发展:基于省市制度互动视角的研究[J].世界经济,2011,(1):126-142

[54]赵群毅,周一星.北京都市区生产者服务业的空间结构——兼与西方主流观点的比较[J].城市规划,2007,(5):24-31

[55]赵群毅,周一星.西方生产性服务业的地理学研究进展[J].地理与地理信息科学,2005,(06):44-48

[56]高运胜.上海生产性服务业聚集区发展模式研究[M].北京:对外经贸大学出版社,2009

[57]原小能,石奇.服务外包与产业结构升级研讨会综述[J].经济研究,2008,(2):158-160

[58] Baumol, W. J. Macroeconomics of Unbalanced Growth: The Anatomy of Urban Crisis [J].The American Economic Review, 1967, (3):415-426

[59] Rubalcaba, L. The New Service Economy: Challenge and Policy Implications for Europe [M].Edward Elgar Press, 2007

[60]杨勇.中国服务业全要素生产率再测算[J].世界经济,2008,(10):46-55

[61]胡朝霞.FDI对中国服务业全要素生产率的影响——基于随机前沿面板数据模型的分析[J].厦门大学学报(哲学社会科学版),2010,(4):115-122

[62]刘兴凯,张诚.中国服务业全要素生产率增长及其收敛分析[J].数量经济技术经济研究,2010,(3):55-67

[63]程大中.中国服务业增长的特点、原因及影响——鲍莫

尔—富克斯假说及其经验研究[J].中国社会科学,2004,(2):18-32

[64] Gouyette, C. and Perelman, S. Productivity Convergence in OECD Service Industries [J]. Structure Change and Economic Dynamics,1997,(8): 222-234

[65]岳希明,张曙光.我国服务业增加值的核算问题[J].经济研究,2002,(12):51-60

[66]江小涓,李辉.服务业与中国经济:相关性和加快增长的潜力[J].经济研究,2004,(01):4-15

[67] Bonatti, L. & Felice. G. Endogenous Growth and Changing Sectoral Composition in Advanced Economies [J]. Structure Change and Economic Dynamics,2007,(43): 79-92

[68]郭克莎.三次产业增长因素及其变动特点分析[J].经济研究,1992,(2):51-61

[69]程大中.中国服务业的增长与技术进步[J].世界经济,2003,(7):35-42

[70]顾乃华.我国服务业发展的效率特征及其影响因素——基于DEA方法的实证研究[J].财贸经济,2008,(4):60-67

[71]杨青青,苏秦,尹琳琳.我国服务业生产率及其影响因素分析——基于随机前沿生产函数的实证研究[J].数量经济技术经济研究,2009,(12):46-57

[72]苗圩.加快推进工业转型升级[J].求是,2012,(3):2-3

[73]国务院.工业转型升级规划(2011—2015年)[EB/OL].(2012-01-18)[2012-03-18] http://www.gov.cn/zwgk/2012-01/18/content_2047619.htm

[74]程大中.中国生产者服务业的增长、结构变化及其影响[J].财贸经济,2006,(10):45-54

[75]姚战琪.工业和服务外包对中国工业生产率的影响[J].经济研究,2010,(7):91-102

[76]顾乃华,毕斗斗,任旺兵.中国转型期生产性服务业发展与制造业竞争力关系研究——基于面板数据的实证分析[J].中国工业经济,2006,(9):14-21

[77]亚当·斯密.国富论[M].上海:上海三联书店,2009

[78]阿林·杨格.报酬递增与经济进步[J].经济社会体制比较,1996,(2):52-57

[79]广州日报.广东求人倍率达1.15-1.18创下新高[EB/OL].(2012-04-01)[2012-02-12].http://finance.huanqiu.com/data/2012-02/2431388.html

[80]麦可思研究院.2011年中国大学生就业报告[M].北京:社会科学文献出版社,2011,77-79

[81]蔡昉.人口转变、人口红利和刘易斯转折点[J].经济研究,2010,(4):4-13

[82]于刃刚.配第-克拉克定理述评[J].经济学动态,1996,(8):63-65

[83]钱纳里等.工业化和经济增长的比较研究[M].上海:三联书店和上海人民出版社,1995,44-49

[84]库兹涅茨.现代经济增长理论[M].北京:北京经济学院出版社,1989,117-119

[85]李江帆.中国第三产业经济分析[M].广州:广东人民出版社,2003,45-49

[86]张淑君.服务业就业效应研究[M].北京:中国财政经济出版社,2006,47-52

[87]王朝明,马文武.中国"民工荒"与经济结构调整——基于刘易斯-托达罗理论模型的综合解释[J].河北经贸大学学报,2011,(6):64-70

[88]陈钊,万广华,陆铭.行业间不平等:日益重要的城镇收入差距成因——基于回归方程的分解[J].中国社会科学,2010,(3):65-76

[89]蔡昉,都阳,高文书.就业弹性、自然失业和宏观经济政策——为什么经济增长没有带来显性就业?[J].经济研究,2004,(9):18-25

[90]陆铭,欧海军.高增长与低就业:政府干预与就业弹性的经验研究[J].世界经济,2011,(12):3-31

[91]刘辉煌,刘小方.我国生产性服务业就业吸纳能力的实证分析[J].东北财经大学学报,2008,(1):22-25

[92]田喜洲.制造业对生产性服务业就业的影响空间与机制[J].华中科技大学学报,2010,(3):73-79

[93]吴淑玲,胡昱.基于生产性服务业就业效应视角的路径分析——以青岛市为例[J].江西社会科学,2011,(8):227-231

[94]Paolo Piacentini and Paolo Pini.The Employment Impact of Innovation: Evidence and Policies [M]. London: Routledge, 2000, 33-39

[95]Gill, I.S. and Kharas, H. An East Asian Renaissance: Ideas for Economic Growth[R]. The International Bank for Reconstruction and Development / The World Bank, 2007, 45-52

[96]陆旸.中国的绿色政策与就业:存在双重红利吗?[J].经济研究,2011,(7):42-54

[97]陆铭,高虹,佐藤宏.城市规模与包容性增长[J].世界经济,2012,(10):47-66

[98]王磊,李慧明.减物质化的研究综述与思考[J].中国地质大学学报(社会科学版),2010,(1):52-59

[99]Von Weizsäcker,E.U.Factor four: Doubling Wealth,Halving Resource Use[M].London: Earthscan,1997,78-86

[100]潘晨,傅泽强.减物质化理论模型及案例研究[J].生态经济,2008,(12):54-57

[101] Clevel and Ruth. Indicator of Dematerialization and the Materials Intensity of Use: A Critical Review with Suggestions for Future Research [J].Journal of Industrial Ecology,1999,2(3): 15-50

[102] Panayotou T. Empirical Test and Policy Analysis of Environment Degradation at Different Stages of Economic Development [R].Geneva: International Labor Office,Technology and Environment Programme,1993,15-19

[103]Peter Bartelmus.Quantitative Eco-nomics:How Sustainable Are Our Economies [M].Netherlands: Springer Science + Business Media,2008,14-23

[104]国际能源机构.世界能源报告(2011)[R/OL].[2012-01-05] http://www.iea.org/w/bookshop/add.aspx? id = 428,2011-03-15

[105]列昂惕夫.投入产出经济学[M].北京:商务印书馆,1980,32-38

[106]来有为等.生产性服务业的发展趋势和中国的战略选择[M].北京:中国发展出版社,2010,15-18

[107] Hofmann W. G. Industrial Economics [M]. Manchesters University Press,1958,48-49

[108]罗斯托.经济增长的阶段[M].北京:中国社会科学出版社,2001,44-52

[109]冯飞,王晓明,王金照.对我国工业化发展阶段的判断[J].中国发展观察,2012,(8):24-26

[110]陈佳贵,黄群慧,吕铁,李晓华.中国工业化进程报告(1995-2010)[M].北京:社会科学文献出版社,2012,77-79

[111]赵渺希,刘铮.基于生产性服务业的中国城市网络研究[J].城市规划,2012,(9):23-28

[112]顾乃华.我国城市生产性服务业集聚对工业的外溢效应及其区域边界——基于HLM模型的实证研究[J].财贸经济,2011,(5):115-122

[113]崔大树、杨永亮.生产性服务业空间分异的动因与表现——一个理论分析框架[J].学术月刊,2014,(3):94-102

[114]赵德海,张永山.服务业发展与创新国际研讨会综述[J].经济研究,2008,(2):155-157

[115]何骏.探索中国生产性服务业的发展之路——中国生产性服务业崛起的动因、空间和模式研究[J].经济学动态,2009,(2):68-72

[116]刘奕,夏杰长.全球价值链下服务业集聚区的嵌入与升级——创意产业的案例分析[J].中国工业经济,2009,(12):56-65

[117]陈建军,陈菁菁.生产性服务业与制造业的协同定位研

究——以浙江省69个城市和地区为例[J].中国工业经济,2011,(6):141-150

[118]江静、刘志彪.世界工厂的定位能促进中国生产性服务业发展吗?经济理论与经济管理,2010,(3):62-68

[119]李强.基于城市视角下的生产性服务业与制造业双重集聚研究[J].商业经济与管理,2013,(1):70-78

[120]王海江,苗长虹,茹乐峰,关中美.我国中心城市生产性服务业对外服务能力的空间格局——兼论与制造业分布关系[J].人文地理,2014,(2):83-89

[121]徐春华,刘力.论生产性服务业的适度规模——基于马克思经济学的视角[J].当代经济研究,2014,(11):48-53

[122]李钢.服务业能成为中国经济的动力产业吗[J].中国工业经济,2013,(4):43-55

[123]江波,李江帆.政府规模、劳动-资源密集型产业与生产服务业发展滞后:机理与实证研究[J].中国工业经济,2013,(1):64-76

[124]黄永春,郑江淮,杨以文,祝吕静.中国"去工业化"与美国"再工业化"冲突之谜解析——来自服务业与制造业交互外部性的分析[J].中国工业经济,2013,(3):7-19

[125]金培.中国工业的转型升级[J].中国工业经济,2011,(7):5-14